SARFAESI ACT-SUPREME COURT'S LEADING CASE LAWS

CASE NOTES- FACTS- FINDINGS OF APEX COURT JUDGES & CITATIONS

JAYPRAKASH BANSILAL SOMANI

ISBN 979-888606026-3

Dedicated

To

All the Past & Present Judges of the Supreme Court of India.

Salute to their wisdom.

Salute to their interpretation of Law.

Salute to their elaborative judgement writing.

Contents

Contents

Preface

Dear Learned Advocates of the DRT, DRAT, NCLT, NCLAT, other Tribunals, High Courts, Supreme Court, Corporates, Chartered Accountants, Insolvency Professionals & Individuals,

I am very delighted to provide you a book on 'SARFAESI ACT'- Supreme Court of India's Leading Case Laws'.

In this book you will get...

1. Name of the Case i. e. Cause title

2.Relevant Sections discussed in the case

3. Hon'ble Judges/Coram of the case

4.Number of PDF Pages in Original Judgement of the case

5. All available Citations of the case

6. Case Note with appeal allowed/ dismissed or disposed off

7. Facts of the case

8. Hon'ble Apex Court's findings, while dismissing/allowing or disposing the appeal

9. Ratio Decidendi if any.

My special thanks to Manupatra, because of their web portal I can compile this book in well manner. I am also thankful to Notion Press to support me to publish & market this book throughout the Country. Thanks to my Juniors, Advocate Colleagues & Insolvency Professional Colleagues to support me in this venture.

Mr Rachit Manchanda has helped me a lot to compile this book.

I hope this book will add some value addition in the wealth of your legal knowledge. Your positive feedbacks will boost me to compile/ write further books & negative feedbacks will improve my skills. Kindly send your valuable feedbacks by email.

Thanks with Regards,

Jayprakash B. Somani

Advocate, Supreme Court of India

Email: jaysomani64@gmail.com

Web Site:www.jayprakashsomani.com

Call: 8384051134, 9322188701, 9318381287

Acknowledgements

Printed & Published by
Notion Press
No. 8, 3rd Cross Street,
CIT Colony, Mylapore,
Chennai, Tamil Nadu- 600004

Managed by
Jayprakash Somani Advocates & Solicitors
Law Firm for Supreme Court of India
Delhi Office
257 C, Pocket 1, Mayur Vihar Phase 1, Delhi 110091.
Call 8384051134, 9322188701, 8459194576, 9318381287
01141051516
Supreme Court Chamber
312, 3rd Floor, M. C. Setalvad Block, In front of 'D' Gate, Bhagwan Das Road, Supreme Court of India, New Delhi 110001
Contact: 8459194576, 9811011747,
www.jayprakashsomani.com

Books are available online at

1. Notion Press: https://notionpress.com/author/jayprakash_somani
2. Amazon: https://www.amazon.in/s?k=jayprakash+somani
3. Flipkart: https://www.flipkart.com/search?q=Jayprakash%20Somani

CHAPTER ONE

Pegasus Assets Reconstruction P. Ltd. vs. Haryana Concast Limited and Ors. 2015

Hon'ble Judges/Coram:

Vikramajit Sen and S.K. Singh, JJ.

Relevant Section:

SECURITISATION AND RECONSTRUCTION OF FINANCIAL ASSETS AND ENFORCEMENT OF SECURITY INTEREST ACT, 2002 - Section 9; , Section 13; COMPANIES ACT, 1956 - Section 529; Section 529A

Equivalent Citation: 2016(159)AIC43, AIR2016SC494, 2016(2)AJR329, 2016 (115) ALR 464, 2016 1 AWC854SC, I(2016)BC389(SC), [2016]130CLA135(SC), [2016]194CompCas310(SC), (2016)2CompLJ273(SC), 2016(2)CTC173, 2016(I)CLR(SC)544, 2016(1)KLJ324, 2016-5-LW274, 2017(1)MhLj1, (2016)1MLJ569(SC), 2017(1)MPLJ25, (2017)185PLR114, 2016 131 RD578, 2016(1)SCALE1, (2016)4SCC47, 2016 (1) SCJ 465, [2016]133SCL491(SC), MANU/SC/1489/2015

Number of pages in the original judgement: 10

Case Note:

Banking - Realization of secured interests - Court interference - Sections 9 and 13 of Securitization and Reconstruction of Financial Assets and Enforcement of Security Interest Act, 2002 and Section 529 and 529A of Companies Act, 1956 - Punjab and Haryana High Court upheld judgment of Company Court - Approved certain fetters placed upon Appellant - Allowed it to exercise its powers as secured creditor under SERFAESI Act and to proceed with sale of secured assets - Delhi High Court differed with the view in similar case - Whether Company Court can wield any control in respect of sale of secured asset by secured creditor in exercise of powers available to creditor under SARFAESI Act - Whether P&H High Court's view was correct in contrast to the Delhi High Court's decision

Brief Facts:

Appeal preferred by Pegasus Assets Reconstruction Private Limited (for brevity, 'Pegasus'), which has been heard as the lead matter, arises out of a Division Bench judgment of Punjab and Haryana High Court dated 15.12.2009 whereby the Division Bench upheld the judgment of Company Court and approved of certain fetters placed upon M/s. Pegasus Assets Reconstruction Pvt. Ltd., while allowing it to exercise its powers as a secured creditor under the SARFAESI Act and proceed with the sale of the secured assets.

The Delhi High Court has differed with the views taken by the Punjab and Haryana High Court. According to Delhi High Court, the company judge or the official liquidator cannot have any say in the sale of secured assets by the secured creditors under the SARFAESI Act. The Companies Act cannot be used to put any fetters on the sale by secured creditors because a secured creditor Under Section 13 of the SARFAESI Act has been granted a right to enforce the security interest "without the intervention of the court or tribunal" in accordance with the provisions of the SARFAESI Act.

Held, while affirming Delhi High Court's judgment

A. The SARFAESI Act was enacted to regulate securitization and reconstruction of financial assets and enforcement of security interest and for matters connected therewith or incidental thereto. Inter-alia, one of the main objects of this Act is to clothe the banks and financial institutions in India with power to take possession of securities and sell them. All its significant provisions have been noted in detail in Mardia Chemicals in which vires of this Act was examined and upheld. A reading of Sections 9 and 13 of the SARFAESI Act leaves no manner of doubt that for enforcement of its security interest, a secured creditor has been not only vested with powers to do so without the intervention of the court or tribunal but detailed procedure has also been prescribed to take care of various eventualities such as when the borrower company is under liquidation for which proviso to Sub-section (9) of Section 13 contains clear mandate keeping in view the provisions of Section 529 and 529A of the Companies Act, 1956.17

B. The above discussion supports the view taken by Delhi High Court that no order is required by the Company Judge for association of the Official Liquidator in order to protect the interest of workers and to realize their dues. Sufficient provisions have been made for this purpose under the SARFAESI Act and the Rules framed thereunder. 18

C. There was clear intention of the Parliament expressed in Section 13 of the SARFAESI Act that a secured creditor has the right to enforce its security interest without the intervention of the court or tribunal. At the same time, this Act takes care that in case of grievance, the borrower, which in the case of a company under liquidation would mean the liquidator, will have the right of seeking redressal Under Sections 17 and 18 of the SARFAESI Act.25

D. The judgment and order of the Delhi High Court is affirmed by holding that powers under the Companies Act cannot be wielded by the Company Judge to interfere with proceedings by a secured creditor to realize its secured interests as per provisions of the SARFAESI Act.[34]

CHAPTER TWO

S. Karthik and Ors. vs. N. Subhash Chand Jain and Ors. 2021

Hon'ble Judges/Coram:

L. Nageswara Rao, B.R. Gavai and B.V. Nagarathna, JJ.

Relevant Sections:

Securitisation And Reconstruction Of Financial Assets And Enforcement Of Security Interest Act, 2002 - Section 13(1), Section 13(2), Section 13(3), Section 13(4), Section 14, Section 17(1), Section 29, Section 35, Section 37; Security Interest (enforcement) Rules, 2002 - Rule 8, Security Interest (enforcement) Rules, 2002 - Rule 8(6), Security Interest (enforcement) Rules, 2002 - Rule 8(8), Security Interest (enforcement) Rules, 2002 - Rule 9, Security Interest (enforcement) Rules, 2002 - Rule 9(1), Security Interest (enforcement) Rules, 2002 - Rule 15; Transfer Of Property Act, 1882 - Section 60, Constitution of India - Article 142, Constitution of India - Article 300A;

Citations:

MANU/SC/0703/2021

Case Note:

Banking - Loan Repayment - Default - Borrower declared Non-performing Asset (NPA) - Proceedings under Securitisation and Reconstruction of Financial Assets and Enforcement of Security Interest Act, 2002 (SARFAESI Act) initiated - Properties mortgaged as collateral security put on auction sale - Several challenges made in proceedings relating to sale of properties concerned - Validity of subsequent sale notices challenged for not giving minimum time period - Whether the proceedings initiated against Borrower sustainable?

Brief Facts:

The present appeals challenged the common judgment and order passed by the High Court in Writ Petition filed by Respondent No. 1, the auction purchaser and in Writ Petition filed by the Appellants herein. In the instant matter, borrower upon failure to repay loan availed subjected to proceedings under SARFAESI Act. It was declared Non-Performing Asset (NPA). In the meantime shares of borrower was already taken over by other concern. However bank still allegedly proceeded against borrower upon guarantors also failing to settle the claims. Dispute primarily relate to sale notices issued in respect of properties mortgaged as collateral security. Appellants contended that Bank did not follow mandatory period of 30 days for the purposes of sale.

Held, while dismissing the Appeal:

Second Sale Notice was in continuation of the proceedings of the First Sale Notice, which sale could not be effected only on account of the interim orders passed by the DRT, Chennai, on the representation made by the Appellants and Respondent Nos. 2 to 4. Since the sale scheduled as per the First Sale Notice could not be held due to the reasons attributable solely to the guarantors, there was no necessity of again following the same procedure of providing a 30 days' clear notice. [60]

The Appellants had ample opportunities for redemption of mortgage, they failed to avail of the said opportunities.[73]

Even otherwise, the claim of the Appellants is not sustainable. The right of redemption, which is embodied in Section 60 of the Transfer of Property Act, is available to the mortgagor unless it has been extinguished by the act of parties. Only on execution of the conveyance and registration of transfer of the mortgagor's interest by registered instrument, that the mortgagor's right of redemption will be extinguished. In the present case, the DRT, Chennai, had granted liberty to the Respondent-Bank to proceed with the sale. The sale came to be registered in favour of the auction purchaser when mortgagor's right of redemption stood extinguished.[74]

The SARFAESI Act was enacted with the purpose for securitization and empowering banks and financial institutions to take possession of the securities and to sell them without the intervention of the Court.[76]

In the present case every attempt has been made to frustrate the purpose of the SARFAESI Act. The Respondent-Bank was required to indulge in three rounds of litigations. [77]

Though the auction purchaser emerged as the successful bidder, in the bids held on 20.7.2012, and though the sale was confirmed on 21.7.2012, and though the sale has been registered in his favour, for a period of last 9 years, he could not enjoy the fruits of the said sale. Not only that, but the Appellants continued to enjoy the rent of the properties, the ownership of which vests in the auction purchaser.[78]

No merit insofar as the challenge to the notice concerned.[79]

Appeals dismissed.[83]

CHAPTER THREE

Sesh Nath Singh and Ors. VS. Baidyabati Sheoraphali Co-Operative Bank Ltd and Ors., 2021

Hon'ble Judges/Coram:

Indira Banerjee and Hemant Gupta, JJ.

Relevant Section:

Securitisation And Reconstruction Of Financial Assets And Enforcement Of Security Interest Act, 2002 - Section 13

Equivalent Citations:

AIR2021SC2637, 2021(3)ALT156, 2021(4)ALD8, 2021(3)CTC681, (2021)7SCC313, MANU/SC/0205/2021

Case Notes:

Company - Insolvency Resolution Process - Initiation of - Sections 13(2), 13(4), 14 and 18 of Securitization and Reconstruction of Financial Assets and Enforcement of Security Interest Act, 2002, Section 7 of Insolvency and Bankruptcy Code 2016 and Sections 5, 14 and 14(2) of Limitation Ac, 1963 - Corporate Debtor was engaged in business of export of textile and garments - Corporate Debtor requested Financial Creditor for cash credit facility which was granted - Corporate Debtor defaulted in repayment of its debt to Financial Creditor - Financial Creditor declared said Account of Corporate Debtor Non Performing Asset (NPA) - Financial Creditor issued notice to Corporate Debtor under Section 13(2) of Act calling upon Corporate Debtor to discharge in full, its outstanding liability - Corporate Debtor made representation to Financial Creditor objecting to notice under Section 13(2) of Act which was rejected by Financial Creditor - Financial Creditor issued notice to Corporate Debtor under Section 13(4)(a) of Act, calling upon Corporate Debtor to handover peaceful possession of secured immovable assets - Corporate Debtor filed writ application in High Court challenging said notices issued by Financial Creditor - District Magistrate issued order under SARFAESI Act for possession by Financial Creditor of assets of Corporate Debtor hypothecated to Financial Creditor - High Court passed interim order restraining Financial Creditor from taking steps against Corporate Debtor - Financial Creditor filed application in NCLT for initiation of Corporate Insolvency Resolution Process (CIRP) against Corporate Debtor under Section 7 of IBC - NCLT admitted application, initiated CIRP, appointed Insolvency Resolution Professional (IRP) - Corporate Debtor filed appeal before NCLAT, contending that application filed by Financial Creditor should not have been entertained, same being barred by limitation - NCLAT dismissed appeal filed by Corporate Debtor - Hence, present appeal - Whether impugned order of initiation of Corporate Insolvency Resolution Process (CIRP) against Corporate Debtor was suffer from any infirmity.

Brief Facts:

The Corporate Debtor was inter alia engaged in the business of export of textile and garments. The Corporate Debtor requested the Financial Creditor for cash credit facility. By a letter of sanction, the Financial Creditor granted Cash Credit Facility to the Corporate Debtor, after which a Cash Credit Account was opened in the name of the Corporate Debtor. The Corporate Debtor duly executed a hypothecation agreement with the Financial Creditor. According to the Financial Creditor, the Corporate Debtor defaulted in repayment of its debt to the Financial Creditor, in terms of cash credit facility granted by the Financial Creditor to the Corporate Debtor. The Financial Creditor declared the said Account of the Corporate Debtor a Non Performing Asset (NPA). The Financial Creditor issued notice to the Corporate Debtor under Section 13(2) of the Act, 2002 calling upon the Corporate Debtor to discharge in full, its outstanding liability. The Corporate Debtor made a representation to the Financial Creditor under Section 13(3A) of the SARFAESI Act objecting to the notice under Section 13(2) of the SARFAESI Act. The Financial Creditor rejected the said representation of the Corporate Debtor and once again requested Corporate Debtor to clear the outstanding amount. The Financial Creditor issued a notice to the Corporate Debtor under Section 13(4)(a) of the SARFAESI

Act, calling upon the Corporate Debtor to handover peaceful possession of the secured immovable assets as detailed in the schedule, failing which the Financial Creditor would be forced to seek the assistance of the District Magistrate, for taking possession of the aforesaid secured assets. The Corporate Debtor filed writ application in the High Court inter alia challenging the said notices issued by the Financial Creditor under Section 13(2) and 13(4) of the SARFAESI Act. While the said writ petition was pending in the High Court, the Authorized Officer of the Financial Creditor issued a notice, notifying the Corporate Debtor, the guarantors and the public in general, that the Authorized Officer of the Financial Creditor had taken possession of the secured assets of the Corporate Debtor. The District Magistrate issued an order under the SARFAESI Act for possession by the Financial Creditor of the assets of the Corporate Debtor hypothecated to the Financial Creditor. The High Court passed an interim order restraining the Financial Creditor from taking steps against the Corporate Debtor under the SARFAESI Act until further orders. The Financial Creditor filed an application in the Kolkata Bench of NCLT for initiation of the Corporate Insolvency Resolution Process (CIRP) against the Corporate Debtor under Section 7 of the IBC. NCLT admitted the application filed by the Financial Creditor under Section 7 of IBC, initiated the CIRP, appointed Insolvency Resolution Professional (IRP) and declared a moratorium for the purposes referred to under Section 14 of the IBC. The Corporate Debtor filed an appeal before the NCLAT contending that the application filed by the Financial Creditor should not have been entertained, the same being barred by limitation. The NCLAT dismissed appeal filed by Corporate Debtor.

Held, while dismissing the appeal:

(i) Section 14 excludes the time spent in proceeding in a wrong forum, which is unable to entertain the proceedings for want of jurisdiction, or other such cause. Where such proceedings have ended, the outer limit to claim exclusion under Section 14 would be the date on which the proceedings ended. [84]

(ii) In the instant case, the proceedings under the SARFAESI Act may not have formally been terminated. The proceedings had however been stayed by the High Court by an interim order, on the prima facie satisfaction that the proceedings initiated by the financial creditor, which is a cooperative bank, was without jurisdiction. The writ petition filed by the Corporate Debtor was not disposed of even after almost four years. The carriage of proceedings was with the Corporate Debtor. The interim order was still in force, when proceedings under Section 7 of the IBC were initiated, as a result of which the Financial Creditor was unable to proceed further under the SARFAESI Act. [85]

(iii) Since the proceedings in the High Court were still pending on the date of filing of the application under Section 7 of the IBC in the NCLT, the entire period after the initiation of proceedings under the SARFAESI Act could be excluded. If the period from the date of institution of the proceedings under the SARFAESI Act till the date of filing of the application under Section 7 of the IBC in the NCLT was excluded, the application in the NCLT was well within the limitation of three years. Even if the period between the date of the notice under Section 13(2) and date of the interim order of the High Court staying the proceedings under the SARFAESI Act, on the prima facie ground of want of jurisdiction was excluded, the proceedings under Section 7 of IBC were still within limitation of three years. [87]

(iv) The Chief Metropolitan Magistrate or the Judicial Magistrate, as the case may be, exercising powers under Section 14 of the SARFAESI Act, functions as a Civil Court/Executing Court. Proceedings under the SARFAESI Act would, therefore, be deemed to be civil proceedings in a Court. Moreover, proceedings under the SARFAESI Act under Section 13(4) were appealable to the DRT under Section 18 of the SARFAESI Act. Argument that proceedings under the SARFAESI Act would not qualify for exclusion under Section 14 of the Limitation Act, because those proceedings were not conducted in a Civil Court, could not be sustained. [99]

(v) Keeping in mind the scope and ambit of proceedings under the IBC before the NCLT/NCLAT, the expression Court in Section 14(2) would be deemed to be any forum for a civil proceeding including any Tribunal or any forum under the SARFAESI Act. [101]

(vi) In any case, Section 5 and Section 14 of the Limitation Act are not mutually exclusive. Even in a case where Section 14 does not strictly apply, the principles of Section 14 can be invoked to grant relief to an applicant under Section 5 of the Limitation Act by purposively construing sufficient cause. Delay could be condoned irrespective of whether there was any formal application, if there were sufficient materials on record disclosing sufficient cause for the delay. [102]

(vii) The NCLAT rightly refused to stay the proceedings before the NCLT. The judgment and order of the NCLT did not warrant interference.

[103]

CHAPTER FOUR

Hemraj Ratnakar Salian vs. HDFC Bank Ltd. and Ors., 2021

Hon'ble Judges/Coram:

S. Abdul Nazeer and Krishna Murari, JJ.

Relevant Section:

Securitisation And Reconstruction Of Financial Assets And Enforcement Of Security Interest Act, 2002 - Section 13(2); Securitisation And Reconstruction Of Financial Assets And Enforcement Of Security Interest Act, 2002 - Section 13(13)

Case Note:

Tenancy - Protection of Tenant - Secured Asset - Maharashtra Rent Control Act, 1999 - Section 14 of the Securitisation and Reconstruction of Financial Assets and Enforcement of Security Interest Act, 2002 (SARFAESI Act)- Borrowers defaulted in loan repayment - Accounts declared non-performing assets (NPA)- Appellant claiming to be tenant in secured asset sought restrain against Respondent Bank from taking possession - Application rejected - Whether Appellant was tenant-in-sufferance and could prove tenancy to claim protection?

Brief Facts:

The instant matter emanated from claim of Appellant, contending to be protected tenant under the provisions of the Maharashtra Rent Control Act, 1999 in the secured asset. Appellant's plea however rejected by CMM court for want of registered/ appropriate proof of tenancy. Hence the present appeal. Bank contended that rent receipts shown were after the creation of mortgage in its favour.

Held, while dismissing the Appeal:

There is a serious doubt as to the bona fide of the tenant, as there is no good or sufficient evidence to establish the tenancy of the Appellant. According to the Appellant, he is a tenant of the Secured Asset from 12.06.2012. However, the documents produced in support of his claim are xerox copies of the rent receipts and the first xerox copy of the rent receipt is of 12.05.2013 which is after the date of creation of the mortgage. It is pertinent to note here that the Borrowers have not claimed that any tenant is staying at the Secured Asset. At the time of grant of facility; third-party valuers had also confirmed that the Borrowers were staying at the Secured Asset. Be that as it may. The Appellant has pleaded tenancy from 12.06.2012 to 17.12.2018. This is not supported by any registered instrument. Further, even according to the Appellant, he is a "tenant-in-sufferance", therefore, he is not entitled to any protection of the Rent Act. Secondly, even if the tenancy has been claimed to be renewed in terms of Section 13(13) of the SARFAESI Act, the Borrower would be required to seek consent of the secured creditor for transfer of the Secured Asset by way of sale, lease or otherwise, after issuance of the notice Under Section 13(2) of the SARFAESI Act and, admittedly, no such consent has been sought by the Borrower in the present case.[14]

No merit in the appeals and thus dismissed.[15]

CHAPTER FIVE

Indiabulls Housing Finance Limited vs. Deccan Chronicle Holdings Limited and Ors. , 2018

Hon'ble Judges/Coram:

A.K. Sikri and Ashok Bhushan, JJ.

Relevant Section:

SECURITISATION AND RECONSTRUCTION OF FINANCIAL ASSETS AND ENFORCEMENT OF SECURITY INTEREST ACT, 2002 - Section 2(1)

Equivalent Citation: 2018(185)AIC170, 2018 (128) ALR 234, 2018 3 AWC2677SC, 2018(2)BomCR739, 2018 (1) CCC 349 , 2018(2) CHN (SC) 201, [2018]143CLA196(SC), [2018]207CompCas586(SC), (2018)2CompLJ145(SC), 2018(4)CTC296, 2018(2)RCR(Civil)323, 2018 140 RD99, 2018(3)SCALE399, (2018)14SCC783, 2018 (4) SCJ 436, [2018]146SCL483(SC), 2018 (2) WLN 1 (SC), MANU/SC/0163/2018

Case Notes:

Banking - Invocation of Provision - Determination - Present appeal filed against order wherein High Court quashed Appellants action for recovery of loan amounts payable by Respondents - Whether order of High Court justifiable

Brief Facts:

M/s. Indiabulls Financial Services Limited (IBFSL) was granted a certificate to operate as a non banking financial company. The Appellant and IBFSL were sister concerns. The IBFSL had disbursed a loan to the Respondent borrowers by creating equitable mortgage over various properties. After sometime the IBFSL gets merged with the Appellant and the assets and liabilities of IBFSL stood vested in the Appellant. The Respondent borrowers had committed default in repaying the loans advanced even before the merger; loan recall notice was also issued. Subsequently, the loan accounts of the Respondents and were classified as non-performing assets (NPA). A notice was issued under Securitization and Reconstruction of Financial Assets and Enforcement of Security Interest Act, 2002 (SARFAESI Act) taking possession over the mortgaged properties. The Appellant issued an auction notice and the matter was adjudicated wherein the High Court quashed the actions of the Appellants for recovery of loan amount holding that the Respondents had not borrowed any amount from the Appellant. The loan was taken from IBFSL, which was not under the purview of SARFAESI Act. Therefore, at the time of taking the loan, the transaction which was outside the purview of the SARFAESI Act, could not be brought under its purview without the consent of the borrower. Hence, present appeal was filed.

Held, while allowing appeal:

(i) In the instant case, loan was given by IBFSL which was not a financial institution covered by the SARFAESI Act when the loan was given. However, this entity got merged with the Appellant and Appellant was a SARFAESI company. The loan/debts/financial assets stood vested in the Appellant pursuant to the amalgamation scheme filed by the two companies where under the predecessor company, IBFSL got amalgamated with the Appellant. Thus, on sanction of the scheme of amalgamation, all loans, recoveries, security, interest, financial documents, etc. in favor of IBFSL got transferred to and stood vested in the Appellant including the loans given by IBFSL to Respondent borrowers, debts recoverable by IBFSL from Respondent borrowers in favor of IBFSL, security documents executed by Respondent borrowers in favor of IBFSL, etc. On the sanctioning of the scheme, the Respondent borrowers became the borrower of the Appellant as if the financial assistance was granted by the Appellant to the Respondent borrowers. The present Court was of the opinion that the aforesaid discussion, thus, leads to conclude that Respondent would be treated as 'borrower' within the SARFAESI Act. [33],[34] and[43]

CHAPTER SIX

Mathew Varghese vs. M. Amritha Kumar and Ors. , 2014

Hon'ble Judges/Coram:

A.K. Patnaik and F.M. Ibrahim Kalifulla, JJ.

Relevant Sections:

Securitisation and Reconstruction of Financial Assets and Enforcement of Security Interest Act, 2002 - Section 13(8)

Equivalent Citation: 2014iv AD (S.C.) 245, 2014(136)AIC15, AIR2015SC50, 2014(4) AKR 530, 2014 (104) ALR 241, III(2014)BC657(SC), [2014]120CLA179(SC), (2014)2CompLJ289(SC), ILR2014(2)Kerala1, JT2014(3)SC151, 2014(2)KLT61(SC), 2014-3-LW289, 2014(6)MhLj34, 2014MPLJ299(SC), 2014 123 RD781, 2014(2)SCALE331, (2014)5SCC610, 2014 (5) SCJ 279, (2014)03WBLR(SC)796, MANU/SC/0114/2014

Case Note:

Securitization and Reconstruction of Financial Assets and Enforcement of Security Interest Act, 2002 (Central Act 54 of 2002) - Section 13(1)--The non obstinate clause in the opening set of expression contained in Section 13(1) is restricted to Section 69 or Section 69A of the Transfer of Property Act, 1882 (Central Act 4 of 1882)--Section 13(1) enables the Secured Creditor to enforce the security interest created in favour of the Secured Creditor without intervention of Court or Tribunal--Transfer of Property Act, 1882 (Central Act 4 of 1882)--Section 69 and Section 69A.

Brief Facts:

The Appeal was filed by the purchaser of a secured asset challenging the judgment of the Division Bench of the High Court of Kerala. The 1st and 2nd respondent stood as guarantors in respect of a credit facility for the tune of ` 30,00,000 granted by the 4th respondent bank in favour of a company. The 1st and 2nd respondent created an equitable mortgage in favour of the 4th respondent bank by depositing the title deeds of their property having an extent of 77.20 cents. Due to the default in remittance by the company, the bank initiated proceedings before the Debt Recovery Tribunal in 2002 for recovery of an amount of ` 33,77,053. The bank also issued a notice under Section 13(2) claiming an amount of ` 70,77,590, the due as on, 11-8-2006. The bank took possession of the mortgaged property by invoking Section 13(4) of the Act. The 1st and 2nd respondent filed an application in the DRT in the pending proceedings challenging the possession notice and also sought for an order restraining the bank from evicting the 1st and 2nd respondent from the property. On 14-8-2007 the bank issued notice to respondents 1 and 2 conveying their intention to sell the property by fixing the reserve price at ` 1,00,25,000. The sale notice was published in leading dailies inviting tenders-cum-auction from the public on 23-8-2007. The 1st and 2nd respondent were informed by the bank of the publication made on 23-8-2007 as per notice dt. 30-8-2007 along with a tender form. The appellant and another submitted their tenders to participate in the sale. The respondents 1 and 2 filed a writ petition challenging the proceeding initiated under the SARFAESI Act. The Single Bench directed the DRT to dispose off the applications filed by the 1st and 2nd respondent without any delay and also gave the parties liberty to settle the liability and directed the bank to defer the sale posted on 25-9-2007 by 6 weeks on condition the respondents 1 and 2 deposit an amount of ` 10,00,000 before 25-9-2007. The respondents 1 and 2 deposited an amount of ` 10,00,000. The DRT thereafter dismissed the application filed by respondents 1 and 2 on 27-12-2007. On the next day the bank accepted the tender of the appellant who offered ` 1,27,00,101 and the appellant was directed to deposit 25% of the amount on that date and the balance within 15 days. The appellant deposited 25% of the amount and the sale was confirmed by the bank in his favour. The appellant subsequently deposited the balance sale consideration. The respondents 1 and 2 filed another writ petition challenging the vires of the Rules on the ground that it violated the right of redemption by denying them adequate opportunity and time to repay the borrowed sum. The writ petition was dismissed on the ground that the respondents 1 and 2 had an efficacious remedy under the SARFAESI Act. Respondents 1 and 2 challenged the order of the Single

Judge by filing writ appeal. In the mean time the bank transferred the property in favour of the appellant under a duly registered certificate of sale. The Division Bench allowed the appeal filed by respondents 1 and 2 by holding that the sale was not conducted in a fair and proper manner and when the initial sale was postponed by 6 weeks from 25-9-2007, the bank ought to have re-notified the sale or at least extended the time for receiving further tenders. The Division Bench set aside the sale already executed in favour of the appellant and imposed a condition requiring the 1st and 2nd respondent to furnish a demand draft of two crores in favour of the appellant within 2 months failing which the appeal would automatically stand dismissed. The time granted by the Division Bench for deposit expired on 8-5-2010. The respondents 1 and 2 did not make the payment within the said date but filed an application seeking 6 weeks further time to effect the payment of two crores to the appellant. The application was allowed and the time was extended to 20-6-2010 directing the 8th respondent, who is a person brought by respondents 1 and 2, to deposit an amount of ` 2,03,00,000 before the bank on 19-6-2010 and directed the sale to be effected in favour of the 8th respondent. The 8th respondent deposited the amount and the bank was directed to execute the sale deed in favour of the 8th respondent. The appellant challenged the judgment of the Division Bench contending that once the sale has been effected and confirmed in accordance with law, merely because someone else has offered a higher amount, the Court should not interfere with the sale as otherwise it would be an unending affair. It was also contended that the jurisdiction of the High Court under Article 226 ought not to have been exercised when there is an alternate remedy under the SARFAESI Act. Rejecting the said contention and dismissing the appeal, it was;

Held:

Under Section 13(1), it is provided that any security interest created in favour of the SECURED CREDITOR may be enforced without the intervention of the Court and Tribunal by such creditor in accordance with the provisions of this Act. The non obstinate clause in the opening set of expressions contained in Section 13(1), as pointed out by Mr. Singh, learned Senior Counsel for the borrowers, is restricted to Section 69 or Section 69A of the T.P. Act. Apart from noting the said statutory impediment, to be noted in Section 13(1), the more important feature to be noted is that a free hand is given to the SECURED CREDITOR for the purpose of enforcing any security interest created in favour of SECURED CREDITOR, without the intervention of the Court or Tribunal. The only other relevant aspect contained in the said sub-section is that such enforcement should be in accordance with the provisions of this Act. A reading of Section 13(1), therefore, is clear to the effect that while on the one hand any SECURED CREDITOR may be entitled to enforce the SECURED ASSET created in its favour on its own without resorting to any court proceedings or approaching the Tribunal, such enforcement should be in conformity with the other provisions of the SARFAESI Act.

Securitisation and Reconstruction of Financial Assets and Enforcement of Security Interest Act, 2002(Central Act 54 of 2002)--Section 13(8)--No sale or transfer of a secured asset can take place without informing the borrower of the time and date of such sale or transfer in order to enable the borrower to tender the dues of the secured creditor--Any such sale or transfer effected without complying with the said statutory requirements would be a constitutional violation nullifying the ultimate sale--Constitution of India--Article 300A.

When we analyze in depth the stipulations contained in the said sub-section (8), we find that there is a valuable right recognized and asserted in favour of the borrower, who is the owner of the SECURED ASSET and who is extended an opportunity to take all efforts to stop the sale or transfer till the last minute before which the said sale or transfer is to be effected. Having regard to such a valuable right of a debtor having been embedded in the said sub-section, it will have to be stated in uncontroverted terms that the said provision has been engrafted in the SARFAESI Act primarily with a view to protect the rights of a borrower, inasmuch as, such an ownership right is a Constitutional Right protected under Article 300A of the Constitution, which mandates that no person shall be deprived of his property save by authority of law. Therefore, de hors, the extent of borrowing made and whatever costs, charges were incurred by the SECURED CREDITOR in respect of such borrowings, when it comes to the question of realizing the dues by bringing the property entrusted with the SECURED CREDITOR for sale to realize money advanced without approaching any Court or Tribunal, the SECURED CREDITOR as a TRUSTEE cannot deal with the said property in any manner it likes and can be disposed of only in the manner prescribed in the SARFAESI Act. Therefore, the creditor should ensure that the borrower was clearly put on notice of the date and time by which either the sale or transfer will be effected in order to provide the required opportunity to the borrower to take all possible steps for retrieving his property or at least ensure that in the process of sale the SECURED ASSET derives the maximum benefit and the SECURED CREDITOR or anyone on its behalf is not allowed to exploit the situation of the borrower by virtue of the proceedings initiated under the SARFAESI Act. More so, under Section 13(1) of the SARFAESI Act, the SECURED CREDITOR is given a free hand to resort to sale of the property without approaching the Court or Tribunal. Therefore, by virtue of the stipulations contained under the provisions of the SARFAESI Act, in particular, Section 13(8), any sale or transfer of a SECURED ASSET, cannot take place without duly informing the borrower of the time and date of such sale or transfer in order to enable the borrower to tender the dues of the SECURED CREDITOR with all costs, charges and expenses and any such sale or transfer effected without complying with the said statutory requirement would be a constitutional violation and nullify the ultimate sale.

Security Interest (Enforcement) Rules, 2002 (Central)--Rules 8 and 9--The requirement under Rule 8(6) and Rule 9(1) contemplates a clear 30 days individual notice to the borrower and also a public notice by way of publication in the newspaper--The use of the expression 'or' in Rule 9(1) should be read as 'and' as that alone would be in consonance with Section 13(8) of the SARFAESI Act--Securitisation and Reconstruction of Financial Assets and Enforcement of Security Interest Act, 2002 (Central Act 54 of 2002)--Section 13(8).

It is, therefore, imperative that for the sale to be effected under Section 13(8), the procedure prescribed under Rule 8 read along with 9(1) has to be necessarily followed, inasmuch as that is the prescription of the law for effecting the sale as has been explained in detail by us in the earlier paragraphs by referring to Sections 13(1), 13(8) and 37, read along with Section 29 and Rule 15. In our considered view any other construction will be doing violence to the provisions of the SARFAESI Act, in particular Section 13(1) and (8) of the said Act.

CHAPTER SEVEN

K. Virupaksha and Ors. vs. The State of Karnataka and Ors., 2020

Hon'ble Judges/Coram:

R. Banumathi, S. Abdul Nazeer and A.S. Bopanna, JJ.

Relevant Section:

Securitisation And Reconstruction Of Financial Assets And Enforcement Of Security Interest Act, 2002 - Section 13; Securitisation And Reconstruction Of Financial Assets And Enforcement Of Security Interest Act, 2002 - Section 14; Securitisation And Reconstruction Of Financial Assets And Enforcement Of Security Interest Act, 2002 - Section 17

Equivalent Citation: AIR2020SC3648, 2020 (2) ALT (Crl.) 97 (A.P.), II(2020)BC52(SC), [2020]157CLA271(SC), [2020]220CompCas505(SC), 2020(2)JKJ365[SC], 2020(3)KarLJ577, 2021-1-LW(Crl)129, 2020(2)MLJ(Crl)54, (2020)4SCC440, 2020 (4) SCJ 657, 2020(2)UC1104, MANU/SC/0257/2020

Case Notes:

Criminal - Quashing of proceedings - Sections 34, 109, 120-B, 405, 406, 409, 417, 420, 426 and 511 of Indian Penal Code, 1860 - Complainant filed complaint in Court of the Principal Civil Judge (Junior Division) and JMFC alleging that Officers of bank in connivance with auction purchaser had caused wrongful loss to Complainant - Complaint being taken on record, Magistrate had referred same for investigation and to submit report - Based on such direction, FIR was registered against Appellants for alleged offences punishable under Sections 511, 109, 34, 120-B, 406, 409, 420, 405, 417 and 426 of Code - Appellants, therefore, claiming to be aggrieved had preferred Criminal Petition before High Court for quashing of proceedings which was dismissed by High Court - Hence, present appeal - Whether impugned criminal proceedings initiated against Appellants liable to be quashed.

Brief Facts:

The Complainant filed the complaint in the Court of the Principal Civil Judge (Junior Division) and JMFC, alleging that the Officers of the Bank in connivance with the auction purchaser had caused wrongful loss to the Complainant. To the said complaint, apart from the Bank, the highly placed officials, the Appellants, the valuers and the auction purchaser were shown as the Accused. The said complaint being taken on record, the Magistrate had referred the same for investigation under Section 156(3) of Code of Criminal Procedure and to submit a report. Based on such direction the FIR was registered for alleged offences punishable under Sections 511, 109, 34, 120-B, 406, 409, 420, 405, 417 and 426 of Indian Penal Code. The Appellants, therefore, claiming to be aggrieved had preferred the Criminal Petition under Section 482 of Code of Criminal Procedure which was dismissed by the High Court.

Held, while allowing the appeal:

(i) The sanction of loan, creation of mortgage and the manner in which the sanctioned loan was to be released were all contractual matters between the parties. The Complainant was an industrialist who had obtained the loan in the name of his company and the loan account was maintained by the Bank in that regard. The loan admittedly was sanctioned. When at that stage the amount was released and if any amount was withheld, the Complainant was required to take appropriate action at that point in time and avail his remedy. On the other hand, the Complainant had proceeded with the transaction, maintained the loan account until the account was classified as NPA. Initially the issue raised was only with regard to the under valuation of the property when it was brought to sale. On that aspect, as taken note the writ proceedings were filed and the learned Single Judge having examined, though did not find merit had reserved liberty to raise it before the DRT, which option was also availed. It was only thereafter the impugned complaint was filed. [15]

(ii) The action taken by the Banks under the SARFAESI Act was neither unquestionable nor treated as sacrosanct under all circumstances but if there was discrepancy in the manner the Bank had proceeded it will always be open to assail it in the forum provided. Though in the instant case the application filed by the Complainant before the DRT had been dismissed and the Appeal filed before the DRAT was also stated to be dismissed the

Appellants ought to have availed the remedy diligently. In that direction the further remedy by approaching the High Court to assail the order of DRT and DRAT was also available in appropriate cases. Instead the Petitioner after dismissal of the application before the DRT filed the impugned complaint which appears to be an intimidatory tactic and an afterthought which was an abuse of the process of law. In the matter of present nature if the grievance as put forth was taken note and if the same was allowed to be agitated through a complaint filed at this point in time and if the investigation was allowed to continue it would amount to permitting the jurisdictional police to redo the process which would be in the nature of reviewing the order passed by the Single Judge and the Division Bench in the writ proceedings by the High Court and the orders passed by the competent Court under the SARFAESI Act which was neither desirable nor permissible and the banking system could not be allowed to be held to ransom by such intimidation. Therefore, the present case was a fit case wherein the extraordinary power was necessary to be invoked and exercised. [17]

CHAPTER EIGHT

Vishal N. Kalsaria vs. Bank of India and Ors. , 2016

Hon'ble Judges/Coram:

V. Gopala Gowda and Amitava Roy, JJ.

Relevant Sections:

Securitisation and Reconstruction of Financial Assets and Enforcement of Security Interest Act, 2002 - Section 13, Section 14, Section 17, Section 35, Securitisation and Reconstruction of Financial Assets and Enforcement of Security Interest Act, 2002 - Section 55(2); Non-performing Asset Act, 2002; Registration Act, 1908; Indian Stamp Act, 1899; Constitution of India - Article 1, Constitution of India - Article 2, Constitution of India - Article 3, Constitution of India - Article 4, Constitution of India - Article 141, Article 245, Article 246, Article 247, Article 248, Article 249, Article 250, Article 251, Article 252, Article 253, Article 254; Security Interest (Enforcement) Rules, 2002 - Rule 8(1), Security Interest (Enforcement) Rules, 2002 - Rule 8(2); Code of Civil Procedure, 1908 (CPC)

Citations:

MANU/SC/0061/2016

Case Notes:

Tenancy - Treatment of protected tenant as lessee - Respondent Nos. 4 and 5 - Approached Respondent No. 1-Bank of India - Financial loan - Granted against equitable mortgage of several properties belonging to them - Including property where Appellant is a tenant - Respondent Nos. 4 and 5 failed to pay dues - In terms of SARFAESI Act, their account became a non-performing asset - Respondent-Bank served notice - On failure of Respondent Nos. 4 and 5 - Respondent-Bank filed application before Chief Judicial Magistrate - Sought possession of mortgaged properties - Properties in actual possession of Appellant - Learned Chief Metropolitan Magistrate allowed application - Directed Assistant Registrar of Courts to take possession of secured assets - Respondent No. 4 served notice on Appellant - Vacate the premises within 12 days - Appellant filed Rent Suit - Court of Small Causes allowed application - Passed ad interim order of injunction - Favour of Appellant - Restrained Respondent No. 4 from obstructing possession of Appellant - Appellant then filed application as intervenor - Stay the execution of order passed by Chief Judicial Magistrate - Learned Chief Judicial Magistrate dismissed application filed by Appellant - Present Appeal - Whether a 'protected tenant' under The Maharashtra Rent Control Act, 1999 can be treated as a lessee

Constitution - Overriding of provisions - Learned Chief Judicial Magistrate dismissed Appellant's application for stay of execution - Held - When secured creditor takes action - Section 13 or 14 of SARFAESI Act - Recovering the possession of secured interest and recovering the loan amount - Not open for Court to grant injunction Under Section 33 - Rent Control Act - Present Appeal - Whether the provisions of SARFAESI Act will override the provisions of the Rent Control Act

Brief Facts:

Respondent Nos. 4 and 5 had approached the Bank of India (Respondent No. 1) (the Respondent Bank) for a financial loan, which was granted against equitable mortgage of several properties belonging to them, including the property in which the Appellant is allegedly a tenant. The Respondent Nos. 4 and 5 failed to pay the dues within the stipulated time and thus, in terms of The Securitisation and Reconstruction of Financial Assets and Enforcement of Security Interest Act, 2002 (SARFAESI Act), their account became a non-performing asset.

On 12.03.2010, the Respondent-Bank served on them notice Under Section 13(2) of SARFAESI Act. On failure of the Respondents to clear the dues from the loan amount borrowed by the above Respondent Nos. 4 and 5 within the stipulated statutory period of 60 days, the Respondent-Bank filed an application before the Chief Metropolitan Magistrate, Mumbai Under Section 14 of the SARFAESI Act for seeking possession of the mortgaged properties which are in actual possession of the Appellant. The learned Chief Metropolitan Magistrate allowed the application filed by the Respondent-Bank and directed the Assistant Registrar, Borivali Centre of Courts to take possession of the secured assets. On 26.05.2011, the Respondent No. 4 served a notice on the Appellant, asking him to vacate the premises in which he was residing within 12 days from the receipt of the notice.

The Appellant fearing eviction, filed a Rent Suit before the Court of Small Causes, Bombay. Vide order dated 08.06.2011, the Small Causes Court allowed the application and passed an ad interim order of injunction in favour of the Appellant, restraining Respondent No. 4 from obstructing the possession of the Appellant over the suit premises during the pendency of the suit. In view of the order dated 08.06.2011, the Appellant then filed an application as an intervenor to stay the execution of the order dated 08.04.2011 passed by the Chief Metropolitan Magistrate. The learned Chief Metropolitan Magistrate vide order dated 29.11.2014 dismissed the application filed by the Appellant by placing reliance on a judgment of this Court rendered in the case of Harshad Govardhan Sondagar v. International Assets Reconstruction Co. Ltd. and Ors.

The learned Chief Metropolitan Magistrate further held that when the secured creditor takes action Under Section 13 or 14 of the SARFAESI Act to recover the possession of the secured interest and recover the loan amount by selling the same in public auction, then it is not open for the Court to grant an injunction Under Section 33 of the Rent Control Act. The learned Chief Metropolitan Magistrate further held that the order dated 08.06.2011 passed by the Small Causes Court, Mumbai cannot be said to be binding upon the Respondent-Bank, especially in the light of the fact that it was not a party to the proceedings. Hence the present appeal filed by the Appellant.

Held, while allowing the appeals

1.The SARFAESI Act, which came into force from 21.06.2002, was enacted to provide procedures to the Banks to recover their security interest from the debtors and their collateral security assets as provided under the provisions of the Act. It becomes clear that the SARFAESI Act is meant to operate as a tool for banks and ensures a smooth debt recovery process. Providing a smooth and efficient recovery procedure to enable the banks to recover the Non Performing Assets is a laudable object indeed, which needs to be ensured for the development of the economy of the Country. What has complicated the matters, however, is the clash of this laudable object with another laudable object, namely, to secure the rights of the tenants under the various Rent Control Acts. Rent Control Acts have been enacted by the different state legislatures to secure the rights of the weaker sections of the society, viz., the tenants.[22]

2.It becomes clear from a perusal of the Rent Control Act that the ultimate object behind the enactment of this legislation is to control and regulate the rate of rent so that unnecessary hardship is not caused to the tenant, and also to provide protection to the tenants against arbitrary and unreasonable evictions from the possession of the property.[23]

3.When one understands the factual matrix in the backdrop of the objectives of the above two legislations, the controversy in the instant case assumes immense significance. There is an interest of the bank in recovering the Non Performing Asset on the one hand, and protecting the right of the blameless tenant on the other. The Rent Control Act being a social welfare legislation, must be construed as such. A landlord cannot be permitted to do indirectly what he has been barred from doing under the Rent Control Act, more so when the two legislations, that is the SARFAESI Act and the Rent Control Act operate in completely different fields. While SARFAESI Act is concerned with Non Performing Assets of the Banks, the Rent Control Act governs the relationship between a tenant and the landlord and specifies the rights and liabilities of each as well as the rules of ejectment with respect to such tenants. The provisions of the SARFAESI Act cannot be used to override the provisions of the Rent Control Act.[24]

4.If the contentions of the learned Counsel for the Respondent Banks are to be accepted, it would render the entire scheme of all Rent Control Acts operating in the country as useless and nugatory. Tenants would be left wholly to the mercy of their landlords and in the fear that the landlord may use the tenanted premises as a security interest while taking a loan from a bank and subsequently default on it. Conversely, a landlord would simply have to give up the tenanted premises as a security interest to the creditor banks while he is still getting rent for the same. In case of default of the loan, the maximum brunt will be borne by the unsuspecting tenant, who would be evicted from the possession of the tenanted property by the Bank under the provisions of the SARFAESI Act. Under no circumstances can this be permitted, more so in view of the statutory protections to the tenants under the Rent Control Act and also in respect of contractual tenants along with the possession of their properties which shall be obtained with due process of law.[24]

5.The issue of determination of tenancy is also one which is well settled. While Section 106 of the Transfer of Property Act, 1882 does provide for registration of leases which are created on a year to year basis, what needs to be remembered is the effect of non-registration, or the creation of tenancy by way of an oral agreement. According to Section 106 of the Transfer of Property Act, 1882, a monthly tenancy shall be deemed to be a tenancy from month to month and must be registered if it is reduced into writing. The Transfer of Property Act, however, remains silent on the position of law in cases where the agreement is not reduced into writing.[25]

6.If the two parties are executing their rights and liabilities in the nature of a landlord-tenant relationship and if regular rent is being paid and accepted, then the mere factum of non-registration of deed will not make the lease itself nugatory. If no written lease deed exists, then such tenants are required to prove that they have been in occupation of the premises as tenants by producing such evidence in the proceedings Under Section 14 of the SARFAESI Act before the learned Magistrate. Further, in terms of Section 55(2) of the special law in the instant case, which is the Rent Control Act, the onus to get such a deed registered is on the landlord. In light of the same, neither the landlord nor the banks can be permitted to exploit the fact of non registration of the tenancy deed against the tenant.[25]

7.It is a well settled position of law that a word or sentence cannot be picked up from a judgment to construe that it is the ratio decidendi on the relevant aspect of the case. It is also a well settled position of law that a judgment cannot be read as a statute and interpreted and applied to fact situations. The decision of this Court rendered in the case of Harshad Govardhan Sondagar v. International Assets Reconstruction Co. Ltd. and Ors. cannot be understood to have held that the provisions of the SARFAESI Act override the provisions of the Rent Control Act, and that the Banks are at liberty to evict the tenants residing in the tenanted premises which have been offered as collateral securities for loans on which default has been done by the debtor/landlord.[27] and[28]

8.As far as granting leasehold rights being created after the property has been mortgaged to the bank, the consent of the creditor needs to be taken. The Court has already taken this view in the case of Harshad Govardhan Sondagar v. International Assets Reconstruction Co. Ltd. and Ors. The Court has not stated anything to the effect that the tenancy created after mortgaging the property must necessarily be registered under the provisions of the Registration Act and the Stamp Act.[29]

9.It is a settled position of law that once tenancy is created, a tenant can be evicted only after following the due process of law, as prescribed under the provisions of the Rent Control Act. A tenant cannot be arbitrarily evicted by using the provisions of the SARFAESI Act as that would amount to stultifying the statutory rights of protection given to the tenant. A non obstante Clause (Section 35 of the SARFAESI Act) cannot be used to bulldoze the statutory rights vested on the tenants under the Rent Control Act. The expression 'any other law for the time being in force' as appearing in Section 35 of the SARFAESI Act cannot mean to extend to each and every law enacted by the Central and State legislatures. It can only extend to the laws operating in the same field.[30]

10.If the interpretation of the provisions of SARFAESI Act as submitted by the learned senior Counsel appearing on behalf of the Banks is accepted, it would not only tantamount to violation of rule of law, but would also render a valid Rent Control statute enacted by the State Legislature in exercise of its legislative power Under Article 246(2) of the Constitution of India useless and nugatory. The Constitution of India envisages a federal feature, which has been held to be a basic feature of the Constitution.[31]

11.In view of the above legal position, if the Court accepts the legal submissions made on behalf of the Banks to hold that the provisions of SARFAESI Act override the provisions of the various Rent Control Acts to allow a Bank to evict a tenant from the tenanted premise, which has become a secured asset of the Bank after the default on loan by the landlord and dispense with the procedure laid down under the provisions of the various Rent Control Acts and the law laid down by this Court in catena of cases, then the legislative powers of the state legislatures are denuded which would amount to subverting the law enacted by the State Legislature. Surely, such a situation was not contemplated by the Parliament while enacting the SARFAESI Act and therefore the interpretation sought to be made by the learned Counsel appearing on behalf of the Banks cannot be accepted by this Court as the same is wholly untenable in law.The Court is unable to agree with the contentions advanced by the learned Counsel appearing on behalf of the Respondent Banks.[32] and[33]

12.In view of the foregoing, the impugned judgments and orders passed by the High Court/Chief Metropolitan Magistrate are set aside and the appeals are allowed. The Court further directed that the amounts which are in deposit pursuant to the conditional interim order of this Court towards rent either before the Chief Metropolitan Magistrate/Magistrate Court or with the concerned Banks, shall be adjusted by the concerned Banks towards the debt due from the debtors/landlords in respect of the Appellants in these appeals. The enhanced rent by way of conditional interim order shall be continued to be paid to the respective Banks, which amount shall also be adjusted towards debts of the debtors/landlords. All the pending applications are disposed of.[34]

CHAPTER NINE

Bajarang Shyamsunder Agarwal vs. Central Bank of India and Ors., 2019

Hon'ble Judges/Coram:

N.V. Ramana, Mohan M. Shantanagoudar and Indira Banerjee, JJ.

Relevant Sections:

Securitisation And Reconstruction Of Financial Assets And Enforcement Of Security Interest Act, 2002 - Section 35; Securitisation And Reconstruction Of Financial Assets And Enforcement Of Security Interest Act, 2002 - Section 13(2); Transfer Of Property Act, 1882 - Section 65-A; Securitisation And Reconstruction Of Financial Assets And Enforcement Of Security Interest Act, 2002 - Section 13(13); Transfer Of Property Act, 1882 - Section 107

Equivalent Citation:

2020(1)ABR297, 2019(3)ACR2729, AIR2019SC5017, 2020(1)ALD13, 2020ALLMR(Cri)580, IV(2019)BC1(SC), 2019(4)BomCR(Cri)732, 2019 (3) CCC 497 , [2019]152CLA298(SC), 2020(1)CTC224, 2019(4)JKJ263[SC], 2019(4)KLT143, 2020-4-LW577, 2020(1)N.C.C.295, 2019(12)SCALE230, (2019)9SCC94, [2019]156SCL510(SC), MANU/SC/1248/2019

Case Notes:

Tenancy - Eviction - Secured asset - Section 14 of The Securitization and Reconstruction of Financial Assets and Enforcement of Security Interest Act, 2002 - Chief Metropolitan Magistrate allowed application filed by Respondent No.1 under Section 14 of SARFAESI Act seeking directions to take physical possession of secured asset mortgaged by Respondent No. 2-landlord with Respondent No. 1-bank in equitable mortgage - Appellant-tenant received legal notice to vacate premises - Appellant-tenant preferred suit before Court of Small Causes in which application for interim injunction was allowed - Appellant-tenant preferred application before CMM whereby CMM rejected application holding that Appellant being tenant without any registered instrument was not entitled for possession of secured asset for more than one year from date of execution of unregistered tenancy agreement - Hence, present appeal - Whether provisions of SARFAESI Act affect right of lessee to remain in possession of secured asset during period of lease.

Brief Facts:

The Chief Metropolitan Magistrate allowed application filed by Respondent No.1 under Section 14 of SARFAESI Act. In this order, the Magistrate directed the Assistant Registrar to take possession of the secured asset mortgaged by Respondent No. 2-landlord with Respondent No. 1-bank in equitable mortgage. The Appellant-tenant received a legal notice from Respondent No. 2-borrower/landlord directing the Appellant-tenant to vacate the premises. The Appellant-tenant preferred a suit before the Court of Small Causes. The Small Causes Court allowed the application for interim injunction of the Appellant-tenant filed in the suit and Respondent No. 2-borrower/landlord was restrained from disturbing the possession of the Appellant-tenant. The Appellant-tenant preferred an application before the Chief Metropolitan Magistrate. By the impugned order, the Chief Metropolitan Magistrate after hearing the Appellant-tenant, rejected the application holding that the Appellant-tenant being a tenant without any registered instrument was not entitled for the possession of the secured asset for more than one year from the date of execution of unregistered tenancy agreement.

Held, while dismissing the appeal:

(i) The bona fides of the tenant was highly doubtful, as there was no good or sufficient evidence to establish the tenancy in the first place. The present case involves a tenant who allegedly entered into an oral agreement of tenancy before the mortgage deed was entered into between the borrower and Bank/Creditor. Additionally, it must be noted that tenancy created under such an oral agreement, results in a fresh tenancy after the expiry of statutory period fixed under the T.P. Act. [26]

(ii) The records also did not demonstrate that the Appellant-tenant has been able to prove his status as a valid leaseholder to merit the protection sought for. Admittedly, an equitable mortgage on the secured asset was created by the Respondent No. 2-borrower/landlord by depositing title deeds with Respondent No. 1-bank. However, the date of creation of the tenancy was not established in the present case. [27]

(iii) It was pertinent to note that at the time when the SARFAESI Act proceedings were pending, the factum of tenancy was never revealed by the parties. The earlier order passed by the Chief Metropolitan Magistrate directing the Assistant Registrar to take over the possession of the secured asset, was silent about any existing encumbrance over the secured asset. It was only after passing of the order of the Chief Metropolitan Magistrate, that the Appellant-tenant started agitating his rights before the Small Causes Court based on a completely different fact scenario, without a whisper of the alleged tenancy under the concluded Section 14, SARFAESI Act proceedings. The Respondent No. 2-borrower/landlord did not even respond to the claims of the Appellant-tenant. The Respondent No. 1-bank had produced multiple records to substantiate their claim that the tenant was nowhere to be seen earlier and that this tenancy was created just to defeat the proceedings initiated under the SARFAESI Act. On the contrary, the Appellant-tenant had failed to produce any evidence to substantiate his claim over the secured asset. In such a situation, the Appellant-tenant could not claim protection under the garb of the interim protection granted to him, ex parte, by solely relying upon the xerox of the rent receipts. [31]

(iv) The operation of the Rent Act could not be extended to a tenant-in-sufferance vis-a-vis the SARFAESI Act, due to the operation of Section 13(2) read with Section 13(13) of the SARFAESI Act. A contrary interpretation would violate the intention of the legislature to provide for Section 13(13) of Act, which had a valuable role in making the SARFAESI Act a self-executory instrument for debt recovery. Moreover, such an interpretation would also violate the mandate of Section 35 of SARFAESI Act which was couched in broad terms. [36]

(v) This case, did not mandate the additional protection to be provided under the Rent Act, to the Appellant-tenant. The lower Courts were correct in ordering delivery of possession to the Respondent No. 1-bank as the tenancy stands determined. [37]

Ratio Decidendi:

The operation of the Rent Act could not be extended to a tenant-in-sufferance vis-a-vis the SARFAESI Act, due to the operation of Section 13(2) read with Section 13(13) of the SARFAESI Act.

CHAPTER TEN

M.D. Frozen Foods Exports Pvt. Ltd. and Ors. vs. Hero Fincorp Limited, 2017

Hon'ble Judges/Coram:

Rohinton Fali Nariman and Sanjay Kishan Kaul, JJ.

Relevant Sections:

SECURITISATION AND RECONSTRUCTION OF FINANCIAL ASSETS AND ENFORCEMENT OF SECURITY INTEREST ACT, 2002 - Section 13

Equivalent Citation:

2018(1)ABR61, 2017(180)AIC65, AIR2017SC4481, 2017 (125) ALR 921, 2017 5 AWC4968SC, I(2018)BC337(SC), (2018)2CALLT42(SC), 2017 (4) CCC 4 , [2018]142CLA115(SC), 124(2017)CLT962, [2018]207CompCas558(SC), 2017(6)CTC542, 2018(I)CLR(SC)1, 2018(1)RCR(Civil)23, 2018 138 RD500, 2017(13)SCALE266, (2017)16SCC741, 2017 (8) SCJ 347, [2017]144SCL220(SC), 2018(2)UC789, MANU/SC/1244/2017

Case Notes:

Banking - Initiation of proceedings - Application of provisions - Section 13 of Securitisation and Reconstruction of Financial Assets and Enforcement of Security Interest Act, 2002 - Appellants borrowed monies for their business against security of immovable properties by creation of equitable mortgage by deposit of title document - Financial discipline was not adhered to, apparently almost from inception, and account of Appellants became 'Non-Performing Asset - Matter went to arbitration on lender/Respondent invoking arbitration Clause - Respondent issued notice under Section 13(2) of Act for one of seven properties - Interim orders were granted by Arbitrator restraining Appellant from creating any third party interest over properties - In order to remove any possible impediment in SARFAESI proceedings, application was filed by Respondent to substitute order of status quo qua parties with name of Appellants/borrowers, which was allowed - Appellants, aggrieved by this order, filed appeal which had been dismissed by impugned order of High Court - Hence, present appeal - Whether arbitration proceedings initiated by Respondent could be carried on along with SARFAESI proceedings simultaneously - Whether resort could be had to Section 13 of SARFAESI Act in respect of debts which had arisen out of loan agreement/mortgage created prior to application of SARFAESI Act to Respondent.

Brief Facts:

The Appellants borrowed monies for their business against security of immovable properties by the creation of an equitable mortgage by deposit of title documents (seven such properties). The financial discipline was not adhered to, apparently almost from the inception, and the account of the Appellants became a 'Non-Performing Asset' ('NPA') within the meaning of Section 2(1)(o) of the SARFAESI Act. The agreement inter se the parties contained an arbitration Clause and thus, the matter went to arbitration on the lender/Respondent invoking the arbitration Clause. The Respondent issued a notice under Section 13(2) of the SARFAESI Act for one of the seven properties. The statement of claim was filed by the Respondent before the Arbitrator and interim orders were granted by the Arbitrator restraining the Appellant from creating any third party interest over the properties. The Respondent issued another notice under Section 13(2) of the SARFAESI Act for two more of the seven properties. Insofar as the arbitration proceedings were concerned, the interim order was confirmed. In order to remove any possible impediment in the SARFAESI proceedings, an application was filed by the Respondent to substitute the order of status quo qua parties with the name of the Appellants/borrowers, which was allowed. The Appellants, aggrieved by this order, filed an appeal which had been dismissed by the impugned order of the High Court. Hence, present appeal.

Held, while dismissing the appeal:

(i) It was trite to say that arbitration was an alternative to the civil proceedings. In fact, when a question was raised as to whether the matters which came within the scope and jurisdiction of the Debt Recovery Tribunal under the RDDB Act, could still be referred to arbitration when both parties have incorporated such a clause, the answer was given in the affirmative. That being the position, the Appellants can hardly be permitted to contend that the initiation of arbitration proceedings would, in any manner, prejudice their rights to seek relief under the SARFAESI Act. SARFAESI proceedings were in the nature of enforcement proceedings, while arbitration was an adjudicatory process. In the event that the secured assets were insufficient to satisfy the debts, the secured creditor could proceed against other assets in execution against the debtor, after determination of the pending outstanding amount by a competent forum. [30] and[33]

(ii) The SARFAESI Act was brought into force to solve the problem of recovery of large debts in NPAs. Thus, the very rationale for the said Act to be brought into force was to provide an expeditious procedure where there was a security interest. It certainly did not apply retrospectively from the date when it came into force. The question is whether, the Act being applicable to the Respondent at a subsequent date and thereby allowing the Respondent to utilize its provisions with regards to a past debt, would make any difference to this principle. [36]

(iii) Similarly, the date on which a debt was declared as an NPA would again have no impact. The provisions of the SARFAESI Act would become applicable qua all debts owing and live when the Act became applicable to the Respondent. [41]

CHAPTER ELEVEN

Authorized Officer, State Bank of Travancore and Ors. vs. Mathew K.C., 2018

Hon'ble Judges/Coram:

Rohinton Fali Nariman and Navin Sinha, JJ.

Relevant Section:

SECURITISATION AND RECONSTRUCTION OF FINANCIAL ASSETS AND ENFORCEMENT OF SECURITY INTEREST ACT, 2002 - Section 13(4)

Citations:

MANU/SC/0054/2018

Case Notes:

Banking - Stay order - Challenged thereof - Section 13(4) of Securitization and Reconstruction of Financial Assets and Enforcement of Security Interest Act, 2002 (SARFAESI Act) - Present appeal filed against order whereby High Court stayed further proceedings under Section 13(4) of SARFAESI Act on depositing required amount - Whether High Court justified in staying further proceedings

Brief Facts:

The loan account of the Respondent was declared a Non-Performing Asset (NPA). Despite repeated notices, the Respondent failed and neglected to pay the dues. Statutory notice was issued to the Respondent. The objections were considered, and rejection was communicated by the Appellant. Possession notice was then issued under Section 13(4) of the SARFAESI Act. A writ petition was filed wherein the High Court stayed further proceedings under Section 13(4) of SARFAESI Act upon depositing the required amount. Hence, present appeal was made.

Held, while allowing the appeal:

(i) It is the solemn duty of the Court to apply the correct law without waiting for an objection to be raised by a party, especially when the law stands well settled. Any departure, if permissible, had to be for reasons discussed, of the case falling under a defined exception, duly discussed after noticing the relevant law. In financial matters grant of ex-parte interim orders could have a deleterious effect and the aggrieved had the remedy to move for vacating the interim order. Loans by financial institutions are granted from public money generated at the tax payers' expense. Such loan did not become the property of the person taking the loan, but retains its character of public money given in a fiduciary capacity as entrustment by the public. Timely repayment also ensures liquidity to facilitate loan to another in need, by circulation of the money and could not be permitted to be blocked by frivolous litigation by those who can afford the luxury of the same. [16]

CHAPTER TWELVE

Suzuki Parasrampuria Suitings Pvt. Ltd. vs. The Official Liquidator of Mahendra Petrochemicals Ltd. and Ors., 2018

Hon'ble Judges/Coram:

Ranjan Gogoi, C.J.I., Navin Sinha and K.M. Joseph, JJ.

Relevant Sections:

Securitisation and Reconstruction of Financial Assets and Enforcement of Security Interest Act, 2002; Transfer of Property Act, 1977 - Section 130; Companies (Court) Rules, 1959 - Rule 9

Equivalent Citation:

2018(192)AIC101, AIR2018SC4769, 2018(6)ALD98, 2019 (132) ALR 792, 2018(6)BomCR318, 2018(4)CGLJ241, [2019]212CompCas516(SC), (2018)4CompLJ237(SC), 2019 143 RD307, 2018(4)RLW3250(SC), 2018(14)SCALE85, (2018)10SCC707, 2018 (10) SCJ 226, MANU/SC/1126/2018

Case Note:

Company - Secured creditor - Substitution of - Company Petition was filed for winding up of one company - Said company entered into unregistered memorandum of understanding with sister concern of Appellant for leasing out its properties to Appellant for repayment of its debts - After winding-up order, secured creditor assigned its dues to Appellant - Appellant then filed company application with prayer for substitution in place of secured creditor - Company Judge rejected application holding that Appellant was neither Bank or Banking company or financial institution and therefore could not be substituted - Appeal against said order was also dismissed - Hence, present appeal - Whether impugned order of denial of substitution in place of secured creditor was sustainable.

Brief Facts:

The Company Petition was filed for winding up of one company The company was also referred for rehabilitation to the Board for Industrial and Financial Reconstruction. During pendency of the same, without permission or knowledge of the BIFR, said company entered into an unregistered memorandum of understanding with the sister concern of the Appellant, for leasing out its properties to the Appellant s for repayment of its debts. After the winding-up order, secured creditor assigned its dues to the Appellant and informed the official liquidator thereafter. Appellant then filed Company Application with a prayer for substitution in place of secured creditor. The Company Judge rejected the application holding that the Appellant was neither a Bank or Banking company or a financial institution or securitization company or reconstruction company and therefore could not be substituted in place of secured creditor for the purpose of the SARFAESI Act. Appeal against said order was also dismissed.

Held, while dismissing the appeal:

(i) The Appellant initially took a conscious and considered stand before the Company Judge, staking a claim for being substituted as a secured creditor under the SARFAESI Act consequent to the assignment of debt to it by the secured creditor. That the claim was not simply with regard to assignment of an actionable claim under Section 130 of the T.P. Act was evident from its own pleadings and the pursis filed by the secured creditor before the Debt Recovery Tribunal. No material had been placed with regard to the orders that may have been passed by the Tribunal on such application. After the claim of the Appellant of being a secured creditor was rejected by the Company Judge, and the Appellant realised the unsustainability of its claim in the law, it made a complete volte face from its earlier stand and surprisingly, contrary to its own pleadings, now contended that it had never sought the status of a secured creditor under the SARFAESI Act. [10]

(ii) The contention of the Appellant that it had never sought substitution as a secured creditor under the SARFAESI Act was additionally belied from the recitals contained in the order. Time and again this Court had held that the recitals in the order sheet with regard to what transpired before the High Court are sacrosanct. [11]

(iii) A litigant can take different stands at different times but cannot take contradictory stands in the same case. A party cannot be permitted to approbate and reprobate on the same facts and take inconsistent shifting stands. [12]

CHAPTER THIRTEEN

Hindon Forge Pvt. Ltd. and Ors. vs. The State of Uttar Pradesh and Ors., 2018

Hon'ble Judges/Coram:

Rohinton Fali Nariman and Navin Sinha, JJ.

Relevant Sections:

SECURITISATION AND RECONSTRUCTION OF FINANCIAL ASSETS AND ENFORCEMENT OF SECURITY INTEREST ACT, 2002 - Section 17

Equivalent Citation:

2019(193)AIC135, AIR2018SC5383, 2019(1) ALJ 357, 2019 (132) ALR 690, IV(2018)BC573(SC), 2019(1)BLJ316, 2018 (4) CCC 105 , 2019(1) CHN (SC) 190, [2018]147CLA266(SC), 2019(I)CLR(SC)140, 2018(II)ILR-CUT599, 2018(4)J.L.J.R.430, 2018(4)KLJ726, (2019)1MLJ788, 2019(1)PLJR47, 2018(4)RCR(Civil)948, 2018(14)SCALE543, (2019)2SCC198, 2018 (10) SCJ 465, [2018]150SCL566(SC), (2018)4UPLBEC3013, (2019)1WBLR(SC)134, MANU/SC/1250/2018

Case Notes:

Banking - Maintainability of application - Sections 17(1) and 13(4) of Securitisation and Reconstruction of Financial Assets and Enforcement of Securities Interest Act, 2002("SARFAESI Act"); Section 13(4) of Act read with Rule 8 of Security Interest (Enforcement) Rules, 2002 - Present matter was against conclusion of high Court that, taking "symbolic possession" or issuance of possession notice under Appendix IV of Rules, meeting with any resistance, could not be treated as "measure"/s taken under Section 13(4) of Act and, therefore, borrower at that stage could not file an application under Section 17(1) before DRT. Whether an application under Section 17(1) of SARFAESI Act at instance of a borrower, was maintainable even before physical or actual possession of secured assets was taken by banks/financial institutions in exercise of their powers under Section 13(4) of Act read with Rule 8 of Security Interest (Enforcement) Rules, 2002.

Brief Facts:

Present matters came from a Full Bench judgment of High Court. By an order of reference, a learned Single Judge noticed divergent opinions expressed by two different Benches of Allahabad High Court on question whether an application under Section 17(1) of SARFAESI Act, at instance of a borrower, was maintainable even before physical or actual possession of secured assets was taken by banks/financial institutions in exercise of their powers under Section 13(4) of Act read with Rule 8 of Rules, 2002 ("2002 Rules"). Learned Senior Advocate, appearing on behalf of Appellants, has placed all relevant Sections under SARFAESI Act as well as relevant Rules under 2002 Rules. According to him, scheme of Section 13 was that a notice of default once served under Section 13(2) of Act might call upon borrower to discharge in full his liability to secured creditor within 60 days from date of notice, failing which secured creditor shall be entitled to exercise all or any of rights under Sub-section (4) of Section 13 of Act

Held, while allowing the appeals

Judgment in Mardia Chemicals had made it clear that, all measures having been taken under Section 13(4), and before date of sale auction, it would be open for borrower to file a petition under Section 17 of Act. [9]

A reading of Section 13 would make it clear that, where a default in repayment of a secured debt or any instalment thereof was made by a borrower, secured creditor might require borrower, by notice in writing, to discharge in full his liabilities to secured creditor within 60 days from date of notice. It was only when borrower failed to do so that, secured creditor might have recourse to provisions contained in Section 13(4) of Act. Section 13(3-A) was inserted by 2004 Amendment Act, pursuant to Mardia Chemicals, making it clear that, if on receipt of notice under Section 13, borrower made a representation or raises an objection, secured creditor was to consider such representation or objection and give reasons for non-acceptance. Proviso to Section 13(3-A) made it clear that, this would not confer upon borrower any right to prefer an application to Debts Recovery Tribunal under Section 17 as at this stage, no action had yet been taken under Section 13(4). [10]

Section 17(3) was a provision which armed Debts Recovery Tribunal to give certain reliefs when applications were made before it by borrower.

One of reliefs that could be given was restoration of possession. Other reliefs could also be given under omnibus Section 17(3)(c). Merely because one of reliefs given was that of restoration of possession did not lead to sequitur that only actual physical possession was therefore contemplated by Section 13(4), since other directions that might be considered appropriate and necessary might also be given for wrongful recourse taken by secured creditor to Section 13(4). [16]

Statement of Objects and Reasons of Amendment Act of 2004 also made it clear that not only did reasons have to be given for not accepting objections of borrower under Section 13(3-A), but that applications might be made before Debts Recovery Tribunal without making onerous pre-deposit of 75% which was struck down by this Court in Mardia Chemicals. One of objects of Act, as carried out by Rule 8(1) and 8(2) must also be subserved, namely, to provide borrower with instant recourse to a quasi-judicial body in case of wrongful action taken by secured creditor. [17]

Section 13(4)(a) referred to right to transfer by way of lease for realising secured asset. One way of realising secured asset was when physical possession was taken over and a lease of same was made to a third party. When possession was taken under Rule 8(1) and 8(2), asset could be realised by way of assignment or sale. Right to transfer could be by way of lease, assignment or sale, depending upon which mode of transfer secured creditor chooses for realising secured asset. Also, right to transfer by way of assignment or sale could only be exercised in accordance with Rules 8 and 9 of the 2002 Rules which required various pre-conditions to be met before sale or assignment could be effected. Equally, transfer by way of lease could be done in future in cases where actual physical possession was taken of secured asset after possession was taken under Rule 8(1) and 8(2) at a future point in time. If no such actual physical possession was taken, right to transfer by way of assignment or sale for realising secured asset continued. [18]

Appendix IV-A which was now inserted by notification dated 17th October, 2018, made it clear that statutorily, constructive or physical possession might have been taken, pursuant to which a sale notice might then be issued under Rule 8(6) of the 2002 Rules. Appendix IV-A, therefore recognised fact that, Rule 8(1) and 8(2) referred to constructive possession whereas Rule 8(3) referred to physical possession. Full Bench judgment was erroneous and was set aside. Appeals allowed, and it was declared that, borrower/debtor could approach Debts Recovery Tribunal under Section

17 of Act at stage of possession notice referred to in Rule 8(1) and 8(2) of 2002 Rules. [25]

CHAPTER FOURTEEN

The Maharashtra State Co-operative Bank Ltd. vs. Babulal Lade and Ors., 2019

Hon'ble Judges/Coram:

Mohan M. Shantanagoudar and Krishna Murari, JJ.

Relevant Sections:

Securitisation And Reconstruction Of Financial Assets And Enforcement Of Security Interest Act, 2002 - Section 13(7)

Equivalent Citations:

AIR2020SC2838, 2020(6)ALLMR300, I(2020)BC3(SC), 2020(2)BomCR124, 2020(III)CLR464, [2020(165)FLR980], [2021(168)FLR317], 2020(2)LLN38(SC), 2019(17)SCALE215, (2020)2SCC310, (2020)1SCC(LS)232, MANU/SC/1671/2019

Case Notes:

Labour and Industrial - Recovery certificate - Dues of employees - Respondent No. 6 had obtained credit facilities from Appellant-Bank and mortgaged its properties in return - When it defaulted on repayment of loan, Appellant-Bank initiated recovery proceedings and took physical possession of mortgaged properties - Respondent No.6 issued notice to its employees directing them to proceed on leave without salary - This was challenged before Industrial Court which quashed notice and held that it amounted to unfair labour practice and directed to pay unpaid salaries - Respondent Nos. 1 to 3 filed application seeking issuance of recovery certificate against Respondent No.6 and Appellant-Bank - Industrial Court held that recovery certificate for unpaid salaries could not be issued against Appellant-Bank - In interim period, one of attached properties was auctioned and sold by Appellant-Bank - Aggrieved by non-issuance of recovery certificate against Appellant, Respondent Nos. 1 to 3 filed writ petition before High Court - High Court observed that recovery certificate should have been issued to Collector and Collector could recover amount from sale proceeds held by Appellant-Bank- Hence, present appeal - Whether High Court had erred in directing issuance of a recovery certificate against Appellant.

Brief Facts:

The Respondent had obtained credit facilities from the Appellant-Bank and mortgaged its properties in return. When it defaulted on the repayment of the loan, the Appellant-Bank initiated recovery proceedings and took physical possession of the mortgaged properties of the Respondent No.6 as per Section 13(4) of the SARFAESI Act. Owing to its poor financial condition, the Respondent No.6 issued a notice to its employees directing them to proceed on leave without salary. This was challenged before Industrial Court. The Industrial Court quashed the notice and held that it amounted to an unfair labour practice. Further, the Industrial Court directed the Respondent No,6 to pay the unpaid salaries on top priority basis from any funds that may become available with it. On the basis of this order, Respondent Nos. 1 to 3 filed a miscellaneous application, seeking the issuance of a recovery certificate against the Respondent No,6, its Managing Director and the Appellant-Bank. The Industrial Court held that a recovery certificate for unpaid salaries of the employees could not be issued against the Appellant-Bank. In the interim period, one of the attached properties of the Karkhana was auctioned and sold by the Appellant-Bank. Aggrieved by the non-issuance of a recovery certificate against the Appellant, Respondent Nos. 1 to 3 filed writ petition. The High Court observed that the recovery certificate should have been issued to the Collector for recovering the amount from the Respondent No,6 and its Managing Director. It was further held that after the auction sale, the Appellant-Bank held the proceeds in trust and the Collector could recover the said amount from the sale proceeds held in trust by the Appellant-Bank.

Held, while disposing off the appeal:

(i) Section 529A of the Companies Act, which gives workers' dues a priority over all other debts, cannot be applied to the instant case in view of Section 167 of the Societies Act.

(ii) Merely by virtue of being recoverable as arrears of land revenue, the employees' dues, in respect of which a recovery certificate had been issued by the Industrial Court, cannot be treated as a paramount charge in terms of Section 169(1) of the Land Revenue Code. Instead, under 169(2) of the Land Revenue Code, they would take precedence only over unsecured claims.

(iii) At the same time, the Appellant-Bank did not enjoy any paramount charge over the sale proceeds either. Instead, as per Section 13(7) of the SARFAESI Act, the sale letter and the sale certificate constitute a contract which displaces the order of distribution stipulated under the said provision.

(iv) The cumulative effect of these documents is that the Appellant-Bank must pay the employees dues out of the sale proceeds from the auctioned property. To this extent, the recovery certificate issued by the Industrial Court may be executed against the Appellant. Further, given the significant delay in payment of the salaries to the employees, such recovery shall be made by the Collector within a period of six months from the date of this order.

(v) All other dues in respect of the secured property, including any unpaid statutory dues in relation to employees (provident fund, gratuity, bonus, etc.) shall be paid by Respondent No. 5 within a period of six months from the date of this order. [14]

CHAPTER FIFTEEN

State Bank of India vs. Santosh Gupta and Ors. , 2016

Hon'ble Judges/Coram:

Kurian Joseph and Rohinton Fali Nariman, JJ.

Relevant Sections:

Securitisation And Reconstruction Of Financial Assets And Enforcement Of Security Interest Act, 2002 - Section 13(7)

Equivalent Citation:

2017(171)AIC209, AIR2017SC25, 2017 (121) ALR 505, I(2017)BC289(SC), [2017]202CompCas249(SC), 2016(4)JKJ32[SC], (2017)1MLJ604, 2017 135 RD545, 2016(12)SCALE1044, (2017)2SCC538, (2017)1SCC(LS)470, 2017 (4) SCJ 254, [2017]140SCL215(SC), MANU/SC/1612/2016

Case Notes:

Civil - Legislative competence - Application of Act - Securitisation and Reconstruction of Financial Assets and Enforcement of Security Interest Act, 2002 (SARFAESI) and Section 140 of Jammu and Kashmir Transfer of Property Act, 1920 (Act, 1920) - High Court held that various key provisions of were outside legislative competence of Parliament, as they would collide with Section 140 of Act, 1920 - Said Act had been held to be inapplicable to banks - Hence, present appeal - Whether SARFAESI in its application to State in question would be held to be within legislative competence of Parliament

Brief Facts:

The present appeals arose out of a judgment passed by the High Court, in which it was held that various key provisions of the Securitisation and

Reconstruction of Financial Assets and Enforcement of Security Interest Act, 2002 (SARFAESI) were outside the legislative competence of Parliament, as they would collide with Section 140 of the Transfer of Property Act of Jammu and Kashmir, 1920. The said Act had been held to be inapplicable to banks such as the State Bank of India which are all India banks.

Held, while allowing the appeal:

(i) Qua the State of Jammu and Kashmir, the quasi federal structure of the Constitution of India continues, but with the aforesaid differences. It was therefore difficult to accept the argument the Constitution of India and that of Jammu and Kashmir have equal status. Article 1 of the Constitution of India and Section 3 of the Jammu and Kashmir Constitution make it clear that India shall be a Union of States, and that the State of Jammu and Kashmir is and shall be an integral part of the Union of India. [10]

(ii) Article 370 begins with a non obstante Clause stating that notwithstanding anything contained in the Constitution, first and foremost, under Sub-clause (1)(a) the provisions of Article 238 shall not apply in relation to the State of Jammu and Kashmir. Article 238 has since been repealed and is not of any importance today. It only referred to the application of the provisions of Part VI to States in Part B of the 1st Schedule. Since the scheme of Article 370 was different, the said Article was stated not to apply. But more importantly, the power of Parliament to make laws for the said State shall be limited, in Sub-clause (b)(i), to the matters in the Union List and the Concurrent List of the 7th Schedule to the Constitution of India, which in consultation with the Government of the State, are declared by the President to correspond to matters specified in the Instrument of Accession. Under Article 370(2), the concurrence of the Government of the State, given before the Constituent Assembly is convened, can only be given effect to if ratified by the Constituent Assembly. This legislative scheme therefore illustrates that the State of Jammu and Kashmir is to be dealt with separately owing to the special conditions that existed at the time of the Instrument of Accession. Under Sub-clause (1)(d) of Article 370, other provisions of the Indian Constitution shall apply in relation to the State of Jammu and Kashmir subject to such exceptions and modifications as the President may by order specify. [13] and[14]

(iii) A constitutional amendment is different in quality from an ordinary law and it is clear that the language of Article 368 proviso and the language of Article 370 are different and have to be applied according to their terms.

[15]

(iv) The State of Jammu and Kashmir is stated to be an integral part of the Union of India, and that the executive and legislative power of the State extends to all matters except those with respect to which Parliament has power to make laws for the State under Article 370 of the Constitution of India. A combined reading, therefore, of Article 370 of the Constitution of India, the 1954 Presidential Order as amended from time to time, and the Constitution of Jammu and Kashmir, 1956 would lead to the following position insofar as the legislative competence of the Parliament of India vis-à-vis the State of Jammu and Kashmir is concerned that all entries specified by the 1954 Order contained in List I of the 7th Schedule to the Constitution of India would clothe Parliament with exclusive jurisdiction to make laws in relation to the subject matters set out in those entries. Equally, under the residuary power contained in Entry 97 List I read with Article 248, the specified subject matters set out would indicate that the residuary power of Parliament to enact exclusive laws relating to the subject matters would extend only to the aforesaid subject matters and no further. Parliament would have concurrent power with the State of Jammu and Kashmir with respect to the entries that are specified in the Presidential Order of 1954 under List III of the 7th Schedule of the Constitution of India. This would mean that all the decisions of this Court on principles of repugnancy applicable to Article 254 would apply in full force to laws made which are relatable to these subject matters. Every other subject matter which is not expressly referred to in either List I or List III of the 7th Schedule of the Constitution of India, as applicable in the State of Jammu and Kashmir, is within the legislative competence of the State Legislature of Jammu and Kashmir. [21]

(v) The word "modification" must be given the widest meaning and would include all amendments which either limit or restrict or extend or enlarge the provisions of the Constitution of India. For this reason also it is clear that nothing can ever be frozen so long as the drill of Article 370 is followed. [22]

(vi) In pith and substance the entire Act is referable to Entry 45 List I read with Entry 95 List I in that it deals with recovery of debts due to banks and financial institutions, inter alia through facilitating securitization and reconstruction of financial assets of banks and financial institutions, and sets up a machinery in order to enforce the provisions of the Act. In pith and substance, SARFAESI does not deal with "transfer of property". In fact, in so far as banks and financial institutions are concerned, it deals with recovery of debts owing to such banks and financial institutions and certain measures which can be taken outside of the court process to enforce such recovery. Under Section 13(4) of SARFAESI, apart from recourse to taking possession of secured assets of the borrower and assigning or selling them in order to realise their debts, the banks can also take over the management of the business of the borrower, and/or appoint any person as manager to manage secured assets, the possession of which has been taken over by the secured creditor. Banks as secured creditors may also require at any time by notice in writing, any person who has acquired any of the secured assets from the borrower and from whom money is due or payable to the borrower, to pay the secured creditor so much of the money as is sufficient to pay the secured debt. It is thus clear that the transfer of property, by way of sale or assignment, is only one of several measures of recovery of a secured debt owing to a bank and this being the case, it is clear that SARFAESI, as a whole, cannot possibly be said to be in pith and substance, an Act relatable to the subject matter "transfer of property". At this juncture it is necessary to point out that insofar as the State of Jammu and Kashmir is concerned, Sections 17A and Section 18B of SARFAESI, which apply to the State of Jammu and Kashmir, substituted 'District Judge' and the 'High Court' for the 'Debts Recovery Tribunal' and the 'Appellate Tribunal' respectively. [32]

(vii) Section 140 of the Transfer of Property Act of Jammu and Kashmir will be respected in auction sales that take place within the State. This being the case, it is clear that there is no collision or repugnancy with any of the provisions of SARFAESI, and therefore it is clear that the High Court is absolutely wrong in finding that as Section 140 of the Transfer of Property Act will be infracted, SARFAESI cannot be held to apply to the State of Jammu and Kashmir. Rule 8 has been noticed but brushed aside by the aforesaid judgment. The High court judgment begins from the wrong end and therefore reaches the wrong conclusion. It states that in terms of Section 5 of the Constitution of Jammu and Kashmir, the State has absolute sovereign power to legislate in respect of laws touching the rights of its permanent residents qua their immovable properties. The State legislature having enacted Section 140 of the Jammu and Kashmir Transfer of Property Act, therefore, having clearly stated that the State's subjects/ citizens are by virtue of the said provision protected, SARFAESI cannot intrude and disturb such protection. The whole approach is erroneous. As has been stated hereinabove, Entries 45 and 95 of List I clothe Parliament with exclusive power to make laws with respect to banking, and the entirety of SARFAESI can be said to be referable to Entry 45 and 95 of List I, 7th Schedule to the Constitution of India. This being the case, Section 5 of the Jammu and Kashmir Constitution will only operate in areas in which Parliament has no power to make laws for the State Thus, it is clear that anything that comes in the way of SARFAESI by way of a Jammu and Kashmir law must necessarily give way to the said law by virtue of Article 246 of the Constitution of India as extended to the State of Jammu and Kashmir, read with Section 5 of the Constitution of Jammu and Kashmir. This being the case, it is clear that Sections 13(1) and (4) cannot be held to be beyond the legislative competence of Parliament as has wrongly been held by the High Court. [40]

(viii) The State of Jammu and Kashmir has no vestige of sovereignty outside the Constitution of India and its own Constitution, which is subordinate to the Constitution of India. It is therefore wholly incorrect to describe it as being sovereign in the sense of its residents constituting a separate and distinct class in themselves. [43]

(ix) Article 35A only states that the conferring on permanent residents of Jammu and Kashmir special rights and privileges regarding the acquisition of immovable property in the State cannot be challenged on the ground that it is inconsistent with the fundamental rights chapter of the Indian Constitution. The conferring of such rights and privileges as mentioned in Section 140 of the Jammu and Kashmir Transfer of Property Act is not the subject matter of challenge on the ground that it violates any fundamental right of the Constitution of India. Furthermore, in view of Rule 8(5) proviso, such rights are expressly preserved. [46]

(x) Having held that the provisions of SARFAESI cannot be applied to the State of Jammu and Kashmir, it is a contradiction in terms to state that SARFAESI can be availed of by banks which originate from the State of Jammu and Kashmir for securing monies which are due to them and which have been advanced to borrowers who are not the residents of the State of Jammu and Kashmir. The judgment of the High Court was set aside. As a result, notices issued by banks in terms of Section 13 and other coercive methods taken under the said Section are valid and can be proceeded with further. [47] and[48]

CHAPTER SIXTEEN

United Bank of India vs. Satyawati Tondon and Ors., 2010

Hon'ble Judges/Coram:

G.S. Singhvi and A.K. Ganguly, JJ.

Relevant Sections:

Securitisation and Reconstruction of Financial Assets and Enforcement of Security Interest Act, 2002 - Section 13; Companies Act, 1956 - Section 529

Equivalent Citation:

2010(96)AIC161, AIR2010SC3413, 2010(5)ALLMR(SC)902, 2010 (5) AWC 5098 (SC), III(2010)BC495, III(2010)BC495(SC), 2011(1)BomCR653, [2010]99CLA14(SC), 2010(2)CLJ(SC)280, (2010)3CompLJ585(SC), (2010)3CompLJ585(SC), 2010(II)CLR(SC)564, 2011(II)CLR(SC)564, 2010-5-LW193, 2010(3)RCR(Civil)963, 2010(7)SCALE696, (2010)8SCC110, [2010]9SCR1, 2010(9)UJ4395, MANU/SC/0541/2010

Case Notes:

Banking - Recovery of dues - Sections 13(2), 13(4), 14 Securitization and Reconstruction of Financial Assets and Enforcement of Security Interest Act, 2002 (SARFAESI) - Appellant sanctioned a loan in favour of Respondent No. 2 wherein guarantee for repayment of the loan was given by Respondent No. 1 by mortgaging her property by deposit of title deeds - Notice issued to Respondent Nos. 1 and 2 under Section 13(2) requiring them to pay the balance amount along with future interest and incidental expenses within 60 days on failure to pay the amount - Subsequently, Appellant filed an application under Section 14 of the SARFAESI Act, which was allowed by District Magistrate/Collector - Notice issued under Section 13(4) thereon - High Court restrained the Appellant from taking action in furtherance of the notice - Whether the Division Bench of the High Court was justified in restraining the appellant from proceeding under Section 13(4) of the SARFAESI Act against the property of Respondent No. 1 - Held, even after receipt of notices under Section 13(2) and (4) and order passed under Section 14 of the SARFAESI Act, Respondent Nos. 1 and 2 did not bother to pay the outstanding dues - Action taken by the Appellant for recovery of its dues by issuing notices under Sections 13(2) and 13(4) and by filing an application under Section 14 cannot be faulted on any legally permissible ground that the appellant could not have initiated action against Respondent No. 1 without making efforts for recovery of its dues from the borrower/Respondent No. 2 - Appeal allowed

Brief facts:

With a view to give impetus to the industrial development of the country, the Central and State Governments encouraged the banks and other financial institutions to formulate liberal policies for grant of loans and other financial facilities to those who wanted to set up new industrial units or expand the existing units. Many hundred thousand took advantage of easy financing by the banks and other financial institutions but a large number of them did not repay the amount of loan, etc. Not only this, they instituted frivolous cases and succeeded in persuading the Civil Courts to pass orders of injunction against the steps taken by banks and financial institutions to recover their dues. Due to lack of adequate infrastructure and non-availability of manpower, the regular Courts could not accomplish the task of expeditiously adjudicating the cases instituted by banks and other financial institutions for recovery of their dues. As a result, several hundred crores of public money got blocked in unproductive ventures. In order to redeem the situation, the Government of India constituted a committee under the chairmanship of Shri T. Tiwari to examine the legal and other difficulties faced by banks and financial institutions in the recovery of their dues and suggest remedial measures. The Tiwari Committee noted that the existing procedure for recovery was very cumbersome and suggested that special tribunals be set up for recovery of the dues of banks and financial institutions by following a summary procedure. The Tiwari Committee also prepared a draft of the proposed legislation which contained a provision for disposal of cases in three months and conferment of power upon the Recovery Officer for expeditious execution of orders made by adjudicating bodies. The issue was further examined by the Committee on the Financial System headed by Shri M. Narasimham. In its First Report, the Narasimham Committee also suggested setting up of special tribunals with special powers for adjudication of cases involving the dues of banks and financial institutions.

After considering the reports of the two Committees and taking cognizance of the fact that as on 30-9-1990 more than 15 lakh cases filed by public sector banks and 304 cases filed by financial institutions were pending in various Courts for recovery of debts, etc. amounting to Rs. 6000 crores, the Parliament enacted the Recovery of Debts Due to Banks and Financial Institutions Act, 1993 (for short, 'the DRT Act'). The new legislation facilitated creation of specialised forums i.e., the Debts Recovery Tribunals and the Debts Recovery Appellate Tribunals for expeditious adjudication of disputes relating to recovery of the debts due to banks and financial institutions. Simultaneously, the jurisdiction of the Civil Courts was barred and all pending matters were transferred to the Tribunals from the date of their establishment.

Held while allowing the appeal,

It is a matter of serious concern that despite repeated pronouncement of this Court, the High Courts continue to ignore the availability of statutory remedies under the DRT Act and SARFAESI Act and exercise jurisdiction under Article 226 for passing orders which have serious adverse impact on the right of banks and other financial institutions to recover their dues. We hope and trust that in future the High Courts will exercise their discretion in such matters with greater caution, care and circumspection.

28. Insofar as this case is concerned, we are convinced that the High Court was not at all justified in injuncting the appellant from taking action in furtherance of notice issued under Section 13(4) of the Act.

29. In the result, the appeal is allowed and the impugned order is set aside. Since the respondent has not appeared to contest the appeal, the costs are made easy.

Ratio Decidendi:

"Where statutory remedies are available under a fiscal statute then exercise of jurisdiction under Article 226 by High Court for passing orders which could have serious adverse impact on the right of banks and other financial institutions to recover their dues is not warranted."

CHAPTER SEVENTEEN

Authorized Officer, Indian Overseas Bank and Ors. vs. Ashok Saw Mill, 2009

Hon'ble Judges/Coram:

Altamas Kabir and Cyriac Joseph, JJ.

Relevant Sections:

Securitisation and Reconstruction of Financial Assets and Enforcement of Security Interest Act, 2002 - Section 13; Securitisation and Reconstruction of Financial Assets and Enforcement of Security Interest Act, 2002 - Section 17, Securitisation and Reconstruction of Financial Assets and Enforcement of Security Interest Act, 2002 - Section 17A; Transfer of Property Act, 1882 - Section 69

Equivalent Citations:

2009(96)AIC161, AIR2009SC3413, 2009(5)ALLMR(SC)902,MANU/SC/1219/2009

Case Notes:

Banking - Secured creditors - Sale of secured assets - Power to DRT to set aside sale and restore possession - Sections 13, 13(2), 13(4), 17, 17A, 17(3) and 36 of Securitisation and Reconstruction of Financial Assets and Enforcement of Security Interest Act, 2002 - Appellant Bank initiated action against Respondent under provisions of SARFAESI Act on default in repayments of loans - Demand notices issued - Possession of secured assets taken - Writ Petitions filed by Respondent dismissed with direction to approach Debt Recovery Tribunal (DRT) - Sale notice inviting tenders for sale of secured assets issued - Writ Petitions filed by Appellant disposed of permitting appellant to sell properties subject to confirmation of Court - Properties sold - Fresh SARFAESI application filed by Respondents - Liberty given to Appellant to resist the same - Writ appeal dismissed by Division Bench - Hence, present appeal - Whether DRT has jurisdiction to consider and adjudicate with regard to post 13(4) events - Held, provisions of Section 13 enable the secured creditors, such as Banks and Financial Institutions, not only to take possession of the secured assets of the borrower, but also to take over the management of the business of the borrower, including the right to transfer by way of lease, assignment or sale for realizing secured assets, subject to the conditions indicated in the two provisos to Clause (b) of Sub-section (4) of Section 13 - To prevent misuse of wide powers checks and balances introduced in Section 17 which allow any person including borrower, aggrieved by action taken under Section 13(4) by secured creditor, to make an application to the DRT having jurisdiction in the matter within 45 days from the date of such measures having taken for the reliefs indicated in Sub-section (3) thereof - DRT vested with powers to declare any such action invalid and also to restore possession even though possession may have been made over to the transferee - Legislature by including Sub-section (3) in Section 17 has gone to the extent of vesting the DRT with authority to even set aside a transaction including sale and to restore possession to the borrower in appropriate cases - Action taken by a secured creditor in terms of Section 13(4) is open to scrutiny and cannot be set aside but even the status quo ante can be restored by the DRT - Appeal dismissed

Brief Facts:

The respondent firm and its sister concern, M/s. Ashok Woodworks, which is also a partnership firm, availed of various loans from the appellant Bank which were secured by movable and immovable assets. The loanee firms having defaulted in repayment of the loans and since their accounts became Non Performing Assets (hereinafter referred to as `NPA'), the Bank initiated action against them under the provisions of the Securitisation and Reconstruction of Financial Assets and Enforcement of Security Interest Act, 2002 (hereinafter referred to as `the SARFAESI Act') and issued separate demand notices to the respondent partnership firm and its sister concern under Section 13(2) thereof on 17th September, 2002, and 21st September, 2002, for the recovery of Rs. 1,56,47,638/and Rs. 1,40,18,468.36, respectively.

Held while disposing off the appeal ,

We are unable to agree with or accept the submissions made on behalf of the appellants that the DRT had no jurisdiction to interfere with the action taken by the secured creditor after the stage contemplated under Section 13(4) of the Act. On the other hand, the law is otherwise and it contemplates that the action taken by a secured creditor in terms of Section 13(4) is open to scrutiny and cannot only be set aside but even the status quo ante can be restored by the DRT.

25. The other point regarding the maintainability of the appeal against the review petition, is of little consequence since the appeal was preferred by the appellants themselves. Having invoked the jurisdiction of the Appellate Court, it was no longer open to the appellants to take a contrary view and to urge that such appeal was not maintainable having been filed against an order passed in a review petition.

26. We, therefore, see no reason to interfere with the judgment and order of the High Court and the appeal is accordingly dismissed, but without any order as to costs.

27. The Civil Appeal No. of 2009 (@ Special Leave Petition No. 3020 of 2009 filed by M/s Vasantha Communications Pvt. Limited and others is also disposed of on the basis of the findings in this judgment, without any order as to costs.

Ratio Decidendi:

"Action taken by a secured creditor in terms of Section 13(4) is open to scrutiny and cannot only be set aside but even the status quo ante can be restored by the DRT."

CHAPTER EIGHTEEN

Baleshwar Dayal Jaiswal vs. Bank of India and Ors. , 2015

Hon'ble Judges/Coram:

J.S. Khehar and Adarsh Kumar Goel, JJ.

Relevant Sections:

Securitisation And Reconstruction Of Financial Assets And Enforcement Of Security Interest Act, 2002 - Section 18(1); Securitisation And Reconstruction Of Financial Assets And Enforcement Of Security Interest Act, 2002 - Section 18(2); RECOVERY OF DEBTS AND BANKRUPTCY ACT, 1993 - Section 20(3)

Equivalent Citation:

2015(5)ABR505, 2015VIII AD (S.C.) 645, 2015(153)AIC255, AIR2015SC2881, 2015(4)AJR261, 2015(5)ALD162, 2015 (112) ALR 645, 2015 (5) AWC 4361 (SC), IV(2015)BC182(SC), 2015(4)BLJ35, (2016)2CALLT1(SC), 2015(3)CDR671(SC), 2015(4) CHN (SC) 197, [2015]127CLA461(SC), 2015(3)CLJ(SC)1, 121(2016)CLT26, [2015]192CompCas74(SC), (2015)3CompLJ530(SC), 2015(4)CTC809, 2015(II)CLR(SC)499, 2015(3)J.L.J.R.445, 2015(3)KLJ791, 2015(3)KLT652, 2016-2-LW97, 2016(4)MhLj733, (2015)6MLJ95(SC), 2016(3)MPLJ260, 2015(4)PLJR99, 2015(4)RCR(Civil)801, 2015 129 RD587, 2015(8)SCALE509, (2016)1SCC444, [2015]132SCL129(SC), MANU/SC/0835/2015

Case Notes:

Banking - Section 18(1) Securitisation and Reconstruction of Financial Assets and Enforcement of Security Interest Act, 2002 and Section 20(3) Recovery of Debts Due to Banks and Financial Institutions Act, 1993 - Whether the Appellate Tribunal has the power to condone delay in filing an appeal under Section 18(1) Act, 2002

Civil - Section 29(2) Limitation Act, 1963 - Whether the Appellate Tribunal under the SARFAESI Act was not a Court and therefore, Section 29(2) of the Act, 1963 was not attracted

Brief Facts

Section 18 Act, 2002: Appeal to Appellate Tribunal

(1) Any person aggrieved, by any order made by the Debts Recovery Tribunal Under Section 17 may prefer an appeal alongwith such fee, as may be prescribed to an Appellate Tribunal within thirty days from the date of receipt of the order of Debts Recovery Tribunal

(2) Save as otherwise provided in this Act, the Appellate Tribunal shall, as far as may be, dispose of the appeal in accordance with the provisions of the Recovery of Debts Due to Banks and Financial Institutions Act, 1993 (51 of 1993) and rules made thereunder.

Section 20(3) Act, 1993: Appeal to the Appellate Tribunal

(3) Every appeal Under Sub-section (1) shall be filed within a period of forty-five days from the date on which a copy of the order made, or deemed to have been made, by the Tribunal is received by him and it shall be in such form and be accompanied by such fee as may be prescribed:

Provided that the Appellate Tribunal may entertain an appeal after the expiry of the said period of forty-five days if it is satisfied that there was sufficient cause for not filing it within that period.

Section 29 Act, 1963: Savings

(2) Where any special or local law prescribes for any suit, appeal or application a period of limitation different from the period prescribed by the Schedule, the provisions of Section 3 shall apply as if such period were the period prescribed by the Schedule and for the purpose of determining any period of limitation prescribed for any suit, appeal or application by any special or local law, the provisions contained in Sections 4 to 24 (inclusive) shall apply only in so far as, and to the extent to which, they are not expressly excluded by such special or local law.

Held, disposing off the appeals

1.Section 18(2) Act, 2002 makes clear that the Appellate Tribunal under the Act, 2002 has to dispose of an appeal in accordance with the provisions of the Act, 1993. The provisions of the Act, 1993 are incorporated in the Act, 2002 for disposal of an appeal. It is held that the Appellate Tribunal under the Act, 2002 has the power to condone the delay in filing an appeal before it by virtue of Section 18(2) of the Act, 2002 and proviso to Section 20(3) of the Act, 1993.[8]

2.The period of limitation for filing an appeal under Section 18 of the Act, 2002 is 30 days as against 45 days under Section 20 of the Act, 1993. To this extent, legislative intent may be deliberate. The absence of an express provision for condonation, when Section 18(2) Act, 2002 expressly adopts and incorporates the provisions of the Act, 1993 which contains provision for condonation of delay in filing of an appeal, cannot be read as excluding the power of condonation. The proviso to Section 20(3) Act, 1993 is extended to an appeal under the Act, 2002. Excluding the proviso to Section 20(3) Act, 1993 will be nullifying Section 18(2) of the Act, 2002.[11]

3.The question whether the Tribunal under the Act, 2002 and Act, 1993 was a Court for purposes of Section 29(2) of the Act, 1963 is not delved into. The power of condonation of delay was expressly applicable by virtue of Section 18(2) of the Act, 2002 read with Section 20(3) Act, 1993, and to that extent the provisions of the Act, 1963 having been expressly incorporated under the special statutes in question, Section 29(2) stands impliedly excluded. It is also algreed with the principle that even though Section 5 of the Act, 1993 may be impliedly inapplicable, principle of Section 14 of the Act, 1963 can be held to be applicable even if Section 29(2) of the Act, 1963 does not apply.[14]

CHAPTER NINETEEN

State Bank of India vs. V. Ramakrishnan and Ors. 2018

Hon'ble Judges/Coram:

Rohinton Fali Nariman and Indu Malhotra, JJ.

Relevant Sections:

Securitisation and Reconstruction of Financial Assets and Enforcement of Security Interest Act, 2002 - Section 13, Securitisation and Reconstruction of Financial Assets and Enforcement of Security Interest Act, 2002 - Section 13(2), Securitisation and Reconstruction of Financial Assets and Enforcement of Security Interest Act, 2002 - Section 13(4); Indian Contract Act, 1872 - Section 128

Equivalent Citation:

2018(6)ABR42, 2018(191)AIC239, AIR2018SC3876, 2018(5)ALD162, III(2018)BC593(SC), 2018(6)BomCR47, [2018]145CLA447(SC), [2018]210CompCas364(SC), (2018)4CompLJ48(SC), 2019(1)CTC889, 2019(I)CLR(SC)245, 2018(5)MhLj692, 2018(4)MPLJ23, 2018(4)RCR(Civil)110, 2018(9)SCALE597, 2018 (7) SCJ 632, [2018]149SCL107(SC), MANU/SC/0849/2018

Case Notes:

Banking - Personal guarantor - Applicability of provision - Sections 14,60(2),96 and 101 of Insolvency and Bankruptcy Code, 2016 - Respondent No. 1 was personal guarantor in respect of credit facilities availed by Respondent No. 2 - Respondent No. 2 Company did not pay its debts and application to initiate corporate insolvency resolution process against itself, was admitted - Application was filed by Respondent No. 1 as personal guarantor, with plea that Section 14 of Code would apply to personal guarantor as well - Tribunal allowed application which was confirmed by Appellate Tribunal - Hence, present appeal - Whether Section

14 of Code, would apply to personal guarantor of corporate debtor.

Brief Facts:

Respondent No. 1 was the Managing Director of the corporate debtor, namely, the Respondent No. 2 Company, and also the personal guarantor in respect of credit facilities that had been availed from the Appellant. Respondent No. 2 Company did not pay its debts in time. An application was filed by Respondent No. 2, the corporate debtor, under Section 10 of the Code to initiate the corporate insolvency resolution process against itself, which was admitted. Application was filed by Respondent No. 1 as personal guarantor to the corporate debtor, in which Respondent No. 1 took up the plea that Section 14 of the Code would apply to the personal guarantor as well. Tribunal, held that since under Section 31 of the Code, a Resolution Plan made thereunder would bind the personal guarantor as well, and since, after the creditor is proceeded against, the guarantor stands in the shoes of the creditor, Section 14 would apply in favour of the personal guarantor as well. An appeal filed to the National Company Law Appellate Tribunal resulted in the appeal being dismissed.

Held, while allowing the appeal:

(i) Sub-section (2) of Section 60 of Code speaks of an application relating to the bankruptcy of a personal guarantor of a corporate debtor and states that any such bankruptcy proceedings shall be filed only before the National Company Law Tribunal. The argument of the Respondents that bankruptcy would include SARFAESI proceedings must be turned down as bankruptcy had reference only to the two Insolvency Acts. Thus, SARFAESI proceedings against the guarantor could continue under the SARFAESI Act. Similarly, Sub-section (3) speaks of a bankruptcy proceeding of a personal guarantor of the corporate debtor pending in any Court or Tribunal, which shall stand transferred to the Adjudicating Authority dealing with the insolvency resolution process or liquidation proceedings of such corporate debtor. An Adjudicating Authority, defined under Section 5(1) of the Code, means the National Company Law Tribunal constituted under the Companies Act, 2013. [20]

(ii) Sections 96 and 101 of Code, when contrasted with Section 14 of Code, would show that Section 14 of Code could not possibly apply to a personal guarantor. When an application was filed under Part III, an interim-moratorium or a moratorium was applicable in respect of any debt due. First and foremost, this was a separate moratorium, applicable separately in the case of personal guarantors against whom insolvency resolution processes may be initiated under Part III. Secondly, the protection of the moratorium under these Sections was far greater than that of Section 14 of Code in that pending legal proceedings in respect of the debt and not the debtor are stayed. The difference in language between Sections 14 and 101 of Code was for a reason. Section 14 of Code refers only to debts due by corporate debtors, who are limited liability companies, and it was clear that in the vast majority of cases, personal guarantees are given by Directors who are in management of the companies. The object of the Code was not to allow such guarantors to escape from an independent and co-extensive liability to pay off the entire outstanding debt, which was why Section 14 of Code was not applied to them. [23]

CHAPTER TWENTY

Suman Chadha and Ors. vs. Central Bank of India 2021

Hon'ble Judges/Coram:

Indira Banerjee and V. Ramasubramanian, JJ.

Relevant Sections:

Securitisation And Reconstruction Of Financial Assets And Enforcement Of Security Interest Act, 2002 - Section 13(2), Securitisation And Reconstruction Of Financial Assets And Enforcement Of Security Interest Act, 2002 - Section 13(4), Securitisation And Reconstruction Of Financial Assets And Enforcement Of Security Interest Act, 2002 - Section 17, Constitution of India - Article 136; Contempt Of Courts Act, 1971 - Section 2(b), Contempt Of Courts Act, 1971 - Section 10, Contempt Of Courts Act, 1971 - Section 12, Contempt Of Courts Act, 1971 - Section 13(a), Contempt Of Courts Act, 1971 - Section 19;

Citations:

MANU/SC/0512/2021

Case Notes:

Contempt of Court - Wilful disobedience - Undertaking given before Court - Sections 10 and 12 of the Contempt of Courts Act, 1971 (Act) - Petitioners held guilty of wilfully disobeying undertaking given before Court - Punishment in form of imprisonment and fine directed - Order confirmed by Appellate Court as well - Hence, the present appeal - Whether order holding Petitioners guilty of committing contempt of court sustainable?

Brief Facts:

Petitioners were Directors of a company which availed loan/credit facilities from the Respondent Bank. Their loan account was categorized as a Non Performing Asset due to defaults in repayment. Recovery notice followed by possession notice was issued under the provisions of SARFAESI Act. In rounds of litigation, Petitioners secured a conditional order of stay requiring them to deposit a sum of within stipulated time frame. Petitioners while admitting liability offered, by way of a statement under oath, to deposit 25% of the notice amount in three instalments on or before stipulated date. Cheques given bounced. Respondent-Bank filed a petition under Sections 10 and 12 of the Contempt of Courts Act, 1971 for against Petitioners for wilful and deliberate breach of their undertaking. Petitioners were held guilty of contempt and sentenced for three months imprisonment with fine. Division Bench upheld the order and hence, the present appeal.

Held, while dismissing the Appeals:

Undertaking given by the first Petitioner was also accompanied by an affidavit sworn to by the second Petitioner. In the said affidavit, it was stated by the second Petitioner that her husband has made a statement before the Court which she had understood from him and that she and her husband undertake to abide by the same.[13]

High Court order was passed on the basis of an offer made by the Petitioners, the first of whom was actually present in Court. The offer so made was accepted by the Bank and hence the order was actually based upon the consent of parties.[15]

In this case, the series of acts committed by the Petitioners (i) in issuing post-dated cheques, which were dated beyond the date within which they had agreed to make payment; (ii) in allowing those cheques to be dishonoured; (iii) in not appearing before the Court on the first date of hearing with an excuse that was found to be false; (iv) in coming up with an explanation about their own debtors committing default; and (v) in getting exposed through the report of the SFIO, convinced the High Court to believe that the undertaking given by the Petitioners on 08.04.2015 was not based upon good faith but intended to hoodwink the Court. Therefore, no fault could be found with the High Court holding the Petitioners guilty of contempt.[27]

Finding of the High Court that the Petitioners are guilty of contempt, does not call for interference under Article 136. [31]

Petitioners are guilty of contempt of court, however reducing the period of sentence from three months to the period of imprisonment already suffered/undergone by the Petitioners. [34]

CHAPTER TWENTY-ONE

Agarwal Tracom Pvt. Ltd. vs. Punjab National Bank and Ors., 2017

Hon'ble Judges/Coram:

R.K. Agrawal and Abhay Manohar Sapre, JJ.

Relevant Sections:

SECURITISATION AND RECONSTRUCTION OF FINANCIAL ASSETS AND ENFORCEMENT OF SECURITY INTEREST ACT, 2002 - Section 13; SECURITISATION AND RECONSTRUCTION OF FINANCIAL ASSETS AND ENFORCEMENT OF SECURITY INTEREST ACT, 2002 - Section 17

Equivalent Citation:

2018(181)AIC229, AIR2017SC5562, 2018(6)ALLMR969, 2018 (126) ALR 472, I(2018)BC3(SC), 2018(2)BomCR16, 2017 (4) CCC 467 , 2018(1) CHN (SC) 81, [2018]143CLA218(SC), (2018)1CompLJ1(SC), 2018(I)CLR(SC)439, 2018(1)J.L.J.R.27, 2017(4)KLT1131, 2018-2-LW523, 2018(3)MhLj645, 2018(2)MPLJ648, 2018(1)PLJR102, 2018(1)RCR(Civil)88, 2018 138 RD643, 2017(13)SCALE664, (2018)1SCC626, 2018 (1) SCJ 14, [2018]145SCL83(SC), 2018(2)UC875, MANU/SC/1494/2017

Case Notes:

Banking - Alternative remedy - Validity thereof - Sections 13 and 17 of Securitization and Reconstruction of Financial Assets and Enforcement of Security Interest Act, 2002 - Present appeal filed against order whereby Appellant's petition was dismissed on ground of availability of alternative statutory remedy of filing application under Section 17 of Act to challenge action of Respondent in forfeiting deposit money of Appellant - Whether High Court was justified in holding that remedy of Appellant lied in challenging action of Respondent in forfeiting deposit by filing application under Section 17 of Act before DRT

Brief Facts:

Appellant was a bidder who failed to pay the regular installments towards sale money in terms of memorandum of understanding to Respondent. Dispute arose between Appellant and Respondent before Debt Recovery Tribunal (DRT) wherein an order was passed directing the Appellant not to remove any material from the factory premises. That led the Respondent to forfeit the Appellant's deposit which was challenged in High Court. High Court dismissed the Appellant's petition on the ground of availability of alternative statutory remedy to the Appellant of filing the application under Section 17 of SARFAESI Act before DRT to challenge the action of Respondent in forfeiting the deposit money of the Appellant. Hence, present appeal was filed by Appellant.

Held, while dismissing the appeal:

(i) An action of Respondent in forfeiting the deposit made by Appellant was part of the measures taken by Respondent under Section 13(4). Measures taken under Section 13 (4) would not be completed unless the entire procedure laid down in Rules 8 and 9 for sale of secured assets was fully complied with by the Respondent. Tribunal had been empowered by Section 17(2),(3) and (4) to examine all the steps taken by Respondent with a view to find out as to whether the sale of secured assets was made in conformity with the requirements contained in Section 13(4) read with the Rules or not. [27] and[28]

(ii) The expression "any of the measures referred to in Section 13(4) taken by Respondent in Section 17(1) would include all actions taken by Respondent under the Rules which relate to the measures specified in Section 13(4). Appellant was aggrieved by the action of Respondent in forfeiting their money. The Appellant falls within the expression "any person" as specified under Section 17(1) and hence was entitled to challenge the action of Respondent before DRT by filing an application under Section 17(1) of Act. Lower Court was justified in dismissing the Appellant's petition on the ground of availability of alternative statutory remedy of filing an application under Section 17(1) of Act before the concerned Tribunal to challenge the action of Respondent in forfeiting the Appellant's deposit under Rule 9(5). No infirmity in impugned order. [30],[31] and[34]

Videos & Tv Shows On Law & Exim

List of some important videos & TV shows on Law & EXIM by Adv. Jayprakash Somani on his YouTube Channel 'Jayprakash Somani EXIM & Legal'

Legal Videos: Hindi -English

1) SLP in Supreme Court / Special Leave Petitions in the Supreme Court of India

2) Transfer of Civil & Criminal Cases by the Supreme Court of India / Transfer of Matrimonial Cases

3) Appellate Jurisdiction of the Supreme Court of India

4) Jurisdictions of the Supreme Court of India

5) Public Interest Litigation in the Supreme Court of India / PIL in Supreme Court

6) Article 32 Writ Petitions in the Supreme Court of India

7) Bail Matters Top 10 Supreme Court Cases

8) FIR Quashing in High Court & Supreme Court

9) Bail & Anticipatory Bail Matters in Supreme Court

10) Insolvency & Bankruptcy Matters in the Supreme Court

11) Insolvency & Bankruptcy Code 2016 Part 1

12) Insolvency & Bankruptcy Code 2016 Part 2

13) Insolvency & Bankruptcy Code 2016 Part 3

14) Corporate Liquidation Process

15) Supreme Court Rules & Procedures Webinar of 2.5 hour on Zoom

16) RDDBFI Act, 1993 (Introduction)

17) The Indian Contact Act 1872

18) Negotiable Instruments Act (Introduction)

19) How to avoid matrimonial disputes& some more videos

20)SEBI Matters in the Supreme Court

21) Matrimonial Matters: Supreme Court's 20 Case Laws

22) Consumer Matters Supreme Court's 20 Case Laws

23) Service Matters Supreme Court's 20 Case Laws

24) How to Search Lawyer for Your Matter

25) Property Matters Supreme Court's 20 Case Laws

26) Bail Matters: Supreme Court's 20 Case Laws

27) Supreme Court / High Court Vacation Benches

28)69000 Teacher's Recruitment Matters of UP Government in the Supreme Court

29) Contempt of Court Matters in the Supreme Court

30) Advocate Act's Matters in the Supreme Court

31) Business Law Matters in the Supreme Court

32) Banking Matters in the Supreme Court

33) Labour Law Matters in the Supreme Court

34) Arbitration Matters in the Supreme Court

35) Careers in Law -Zoom Webinar by Adv. Jayprakash Somani

36) Civil Matters in the Supreme Court

37) Consumer Protection Act | Consumer Matters in the Supreme Court

38) Corporate Matters in the Supreme Court

39) Criminal Matters in the Supreme Court

40) Role of Respondent in the Supreme Court of India

41) Motor Vehicle Accident Matters in Supreme Court with case laws

42) Article 131 Original Suits in Supreme Court

43)PIL in Supreme Court/ Public Interest Litigations in the Supreme Court of India'

44)CAB Citizenship Amendment Bill is not Unconstitutional

45) Supreme Court of India Cases & Process – Marathi

46) Legal Services Export / Export of Legal Services

47) Transfer of Matrimonial Cases by the Supreme Court of India

48) Public Interest Litigation PIL

49) The Specific Relief Act (Introduction)

50) Corporate Insolvency Resolution Process CIRP

51)ABMM's Career 5 - Careers in Law

52) Transfer of cases by Supreme Court

53) Writ Petitions in High Court & Supreme Court of India

54) Supreme Court Jurisdictions - Appeals, SLP, Writ Petitions, Transfer, Original, Review, Curative

55)LEGAL INDIA TV Show: Cases Handled in Supreme Court

56) Corporate Liquidation Process

57) Legal Services Export / Export of Legal Services

EXIM Videos: Hindi -English

1) Yes, I can do Import Export Business Easily! 36 points excellent video in Hindi

2) Yes, I can do Import Export Business Easily! 36 points excellent video in English

3) Import Export Business – Hindi video

4) Import Export Business - English video

5) Export Import Marathi TV Interview

6) Scope for Commerce Students in International Business- TV Show

7) Scope for Management Student in International Business- TV Show

8) Scope for Engineering Students in International Business – TV Show

9) Women in International Business- TV Show

10) How to do Import Export Business Successfully!‘

11) Where one can get full information on Import Export Business?

12) What to do import & export?

13) Import Export Workshop/ Training/Course/ Diploma

14) How to Start Import Export Business & How to grow it. Live Webinar

15) Success Stories & Failure Stories in Import & Export Business

16) For MSME Scope in Export & Import...

17) Exports In Agri. & Food Products – English & some more videos

18) Exports to Dubai, Aabudhabii. e. UAE

19) Jewellery Exports from India

20) How to attend EXIM workshop to become excellent Exporter

21) Import Export Best Training Course – Online & Offline

22) Agri Product Export

23) Scope for Woman in International Business

24) Management Graduates Scope in International Business

25) Pharma Product’s Export

26) Best Import Export Course | Practical Training | Aaronica Global Exim

27) Import Export Business for Commerce Graduates

28) How Do I Get Export Orders? Finding International Buyers

29) What Is APEDA In Import Export Business?

30) Which Is The Best Product To Export From India?

31)EXIM Remark by Manoj Kumar Faridabad

32)EXIM Remarks by Mahesh Telangana

33) What Licenses I Need To Start Import/ Export?

34) How Can I Increase My Import Export Business?

35) Which Is Best B2B Website For Import/Export Business?

36) Export Import Management with Global Marketing

37) How to Start Export Import Business | 51 Points Video

38) Scope for Commerce & Other Graduates in International Business

39)BE A SUCCESSFUL EXPORTER FOR OUR NATION - Marathi video

40) Export of Textile , Cotton, Agri., Food, & other products & services

41) Exports from MP, CG, MH, GJ & CA in Fresh Fruits & Vegetables

42) Exports in Agri. & Food Products- Hindi

43) Start your Online/E-Commerce Business

44) How to Start Export Import Business & Grow it

45) Exports in Textile & Other Products

46) Start and grow EXIM business - Live English Webinar

47)'Import Export Business!' Why, Who, What & How can one do it easily!!

48) Live: Export of Product & Services During & After Lock Down Period

49) Frauds in Import Export Business

50) Import Export for Business Man

51) Import & Export for Women

51) Import & Export for Graduate & Post - Graduate Students

52) Agriculture Exports from India

53) Digital Marketing Setup - Marathi

54)2nd Secret of Successful Businessman

55) Digital Marketing Set up

56) Legal Services Export / Export of Legal Services

57) Export & Import with UAE

58) Service Exports / Exports by Service Providers

59) Import Export Workshop/ Training/Course/ Diploma

60) Exports & Imports with USA

61) Selection on Product for Export

62) Top Products Exported from India

63) What to do import & export?

64)ABMM Career 2 - 'Careers in Business & Industries

65) How to do Import Export Business Successfully!'

66)5 Secrets of Successful Businessman

67) Export from MP, Chhattisgarh & Vidarbha Nagpur

68)EXIM Hindi - Textile & Apparel Export

69)EXIM Hindi - Export Import Practical Training In Delhi, Kolkata, Mumbai and Pune

70) Import Export Business

71) Import Export Business Hindi

72) Import Export Business English video

73) Import Export Business Marathi

74) Women in International Business by Exim Guru Adv. Jayprakash Somani

75) Opportunities in Foreign Trade- Adv. Jayprakash Somani's special interview

List Of Adv. Jayprakash Somani's Books

1. Supreme Court of India's Leading Case Laws on 'Insolvency & Bankruptcy Code 2016'

2. Bail Matters – Supreme Court's Latest Leading Case Laws

3. Arbitration Matters- Supreme Court's Latest Leading Case Laws

4. Property Matters - Supreme Court's Latest Leading Case Laws

5. Matrimonial Matters- Supreme Court's Latest Leading Case Laws

6. Election Matters- Supreme Court's Latest Leading Case Laws

7.SEBI Matters- Supreme Court's Latest Leading Case Laws

8. Banking Matters- Supreme Court's Latest Leading Case Laws

9. Service Matters- Supreme Court's Latest Leading Case Laws

10. Contempt of Court Matters- Supreme Court's Latest Leading Case Laws

11. Consumer Protection Matters- Supreme Court's Latest Leading Case Laws

12. Corporate Law- Supreme Court's Latest Leading Case Laws

13. Supreme Court's AOR Exam- Leading Cases

14. Armed Force Tribunal - Supreme Court's Latest Leading Case Laws

15. Acquittal From 376 - Supreme Court's Latest Leading Case Laws

16. Negotiable instrument – Supreme Court's Latest Leading Case Laws

17. Contract Act- Supreme Court's Latest Leading Case Laws

18. Insider trading- Supreme Court's Latest Leading Case Laws

19. Foreign Exchange and Management Act- Supreme Court's Latest Leading Case Laws

20. Income Tax Act- Supreme Court's Latest Leading Case Laws

21. Company Law- Supreme Court's Latest Leading Case Laws

22. Competition & Monopoly Matters- Supreme Court's Latest Leading Case Laws

23. Compassionate Appointment- Service Matters- Supreme Court's Latest Leading Case Laws

24. Compulsory Retirement- Service Matters- Supreme Court's Latest Leading Case Laws

25. Voluntary Retirement- Service Matters- Supreme Court's Latest Leading Case Laws

26. Removal/Dismissal/Termination from Service- Supreme Court's Latest Leading Case Laws

27. Seniority- Service Matter- Supreme Court's Latest Leading Case Laws

28. Promotion- Service Matter- Supreme Court's Latest Leading Case Laws

29. Equal Pay for Equal Work- Service Matter- Supreme Court's Latest Leading Case Laws

30. Condition of Service- Service Matter- Supreme Court's Latest Leading Case Laws

31. Customs Act- Supreme Court's Leading Case Laws

32. SARFAESI ACT- Supreme Court's Leading Case Laws

These Books are available online at

1. **Notion Press:** https://notionpress.com/author/jayprakash_somani
2. **Amazon:** https://www.amazon.in/s?k=jayprakash+somani
3. **Flipkart:** https://www.flipkart.com/search?q=Jayprakash%20Somani

Printed by Libri Plureos GmbH in Hamburg,
Germany